Splash of *Bourbon*

Kentucky's Spirit

A Cookbook By

David Dominé

McClanahan Publishing House, Inc.

For Don and Chris Lowe, dear friends and good eaters.

International Standard Book Number 978-1-934898-06-2
Library of Congress Card Catalog Number 2009943421

Cover design and book layout by Asher Graphics
Food photography by David Dominé
Bourbon Trail sites and Kentucky landscape photography by James Asher

Manufactured in United States

All book order correspondence should be addressed to:

McClanahan Publishing House, Inc.
P.O. Box 100
Kuttawa, KY 42055

800-544-6959
270-388-9388
270-388-6186 FAX

www.kybooks.com
books@kybooks.com

McCLANAHAN
PUBLISHING HOUSE

Acknowledgements

I would like to thank all the individuals and organizations that helped make this book a reality, including previous cookbook authors and food writers whose works have inspired me. To name some, they are Jennie Bennedict, Paula Cunningham, Marion Flexner, Camille Glenn, Marty Godbey, Cissy Gregg, Duncan Hines, Susan Spicer Lowery, Colonel Michael Edward Masters, Elizabeth Ross, Mark Sohn, Michelle Stone and Sharon Thompson. A huge debt of gratitude is also owed to the many cooks, chefs and foodies across the Bluegrass who shared their stories, secrets and tips with me.

I'd also like to express my gratefulness to those who have provided me with encouragement and support. Some of them are: Chuck and Sheelah Anderson, Alan Arnett, Kelly Atkins, Sheila Berman, Gabriele Bosley, Alan and Anne Bird, JoAnn and Arnold Celentano, the late Polly Clark, Don Driskell, Jamie Estes, Kat Galagher, Ron and Jane Harris, Jesse Hendrix Inman, Gene and Norma Johnston, Kevin Kouba, Mari Lively, Don and Chris Lowe, Frances Mengel, Rick and Jeanine Redding, John Reiliford, Claude David Rodgers, Jerry Lee Rodgers, Sara Rowan, Scott and Sharon Risinger, Marjorie Samper, Lewis Shuckman, Sean Stafford, Miss Wanda Stanley, Rick Tabb, Lillie Arundel, Herb and Gayle Warren, and Earlene Zimlich. Thank you as well to Paula Cunningham, Michelle Stone and all the others at McClanahan Publishing House who have made this project possible, and to Jim Asher for the design and layout of the book.

Special Thanks

I would especially like to thank the people who helped test many of the recipes in this cookbook. They are Kim Crum, Wendy Flowers, Michael and Laura Horan, Dick Harrington, Ron and Jane Harris, Tim Holz, Jane Newsom, Beth Schott, Lynn Shanks, and Silvia Zañartu. I'd also like to thank those individuals in the Tuesday Night Dinner Club who graciously offered to taste many of the dishes. They said it was quite a chore.

I'd like as well to acknowledge the assistance from resources such as *The Book of Bourbon* by Gary Regan, *bourbon.com*, *The Bourbon Review*, *bourbonenthusiast.com* and Ron Givens' book *Bourbon at Its Best*, all of which proved invaluable in verifying and completing my research. Thank you as well to John Rose, author of *The Vodka Cookbook*. In addition, I'd like to extend my gratitude to the distilleries and their representatives who agreed to help me with this project. They are Svend Jansen, Andrea Duvall, Even Kulsveen, Drew Kulsveen, Hunter Chavanne, Justin Gaines, Larry Kass, Whitney Mares, Nick Clark, Angela Traver, Lora Piazza, and Honi Goldman. And, thank you to master distillers such as Jimmy Russell, Jim Rutledge, Harlen Wheatley and Fred Noe who provided valuable assistance in completing this project.

Contents

Introduction

Of all the influences that have shaped the rich and bountiful cuisine of the Bluegrass, one of them has enjoyed a prominent position in the flavors of Kentucky cooking. Bourbon whiskey, that fabled and distinctly American spirit, has nevertheless left its mark on kitchens across the country and has contributed to a rich legacy of regional dining that defies the notion of a homogeneous national cuisine. Spicy and sultry, smoky or sweet, whiskey – like fine wine or cognac – can enhance the natural flavors in a wide variety of foods. Bourbon, with its naturally sweet notes and mellow essence, works as a perfect addition in dessert recipes, but it can add subtle tastes to meat dishes, soups, salads, and even breads as well. Apart from that, byproducts of bourbon distilling such as the spent grains of mash and charred barrel staves can be used to impart an entirely different realm of bourbon flavors to food. Bourbon-inspired condiments and seasonings can also enhance a wide variety of dishes during and after cooking. In short, bourbon has many uses in the kitchen.

Whether you choose to enjoy it straight up alongside a plate of southern fried chicken, or in a marinade for your favorite cut of meat, bourbon whiskey adds a splash of unmistakable flavor to your meal. Dash it into sauces, shake it over steamed vegetables, dribble it into soups or stews – a bit of bourbon makes food taste better. And this book: *Splash of Bourbon, Kentucky's Spirit,* will show you how to make the most of bourbon in your kitchen, while at the same time revealing interesting tidbits about this distinctive American spirit.

Unless otherwise stated, all recipes in *Splash of Bourbon* have been designed for 6-8 people.

5

Cooking with Bourbon

Contrary to what you might have heard, cooking, as a rule, does not burn off all the alcohol in a dish. The longer bourbon is cooked, however, the less alcohol will be retained. The cooking method and intensity of heat will also influence the amount of alcohol that remains. According to the United States Department of Agriculture, you will need to cook something with bourbon in it for 2½ hours to remove 95% of the alcohol. The following chart outlines the evaporation process of alcohol in the kitchen:

ALCOHOL RETAINED	COOKING METHOD
85%	Stirred into hot liquid
75%	Flambéed
70%	Stored overnight, no heat
45%	Baked for 25 minutes, not stirred in
	Stirred in and simmered or baked for:
40%	15 minutes
35%	30 minutes
25%	1 hour
20%	1½ hours
10%	2 hours
5%	2½ hours

An important note about cooking with bourbon:

As with many types of alcohol, bourbon can be very flammable, so cooks should exercise utmost caution when using whiskey or other spirits around heat or open flames. If, in the rare case, something you are cooking with bourbon starts to flambé, don't panic: the alcohol will burn off within a minute or two. Nonetheless, always know where your kitchen fire extinguisher is and how to use it.

An American Spirit

Germany is noted for its beer, and France is known for Champagne. Japan has its sake and Scotland has a reputation for, well, its Scotch. But which alcoholic drink is uniquely American? The answer is simple: bourbon.

Although largely unfounded, legend credits Elijah Craig, a Baptist minister, with inventing the spirit in Bourbon County in the late 1780s, when present-day Kentucky was still part of Virginia. Given that France had helped the United States win the Revolutionary War, the Virginia legislature showed its gratitude by bestowing well-known French names on locations as they were settled in Kentucky. Today, towns such as Paris and Versailles hearken back to those early days – and a section of Fayette County in Kentucky would become Bourbon County, named in honor of the French royal family.

Far away from France, however, farmers in the newly independent country had to eke out a living. Corn was widely planted and abundant, yet it was difficult to transport for sale, especially given the poor condition of roads in those days. Enterprising farmers realized that whiskey condensed the corn into a much more profitable product, with flatbed boats on the Ohio River allowing for easy shipping to ports farther south.

A major stop along the way was the river town

Photos by James Asher

of Maysville, in Bourbon County, where barrels of whiskey produced by farmer-distillers reportedly received a stamp identifying them as Bourbon County Whiskey. Noted for their exceptional sweetness and mellowness, the corn-based western whiskeys distinguished themselves from eastern whiskeys, which owed their flavors to the generally high concentration of rye. The quality of the Kentucky whiskey made it highly sought-after, and over time the name evolved to bourbon.

Today, a glance at bourbon brand names offers a lesson in early American history and Bluegrass geography: Buffalo Trace, Cabin Still, Old Rip Van Winkle, Elijah Craig, Sam Houston, Rebel Yell, and Wild Turkey. With this legacy in mind, the U.S. Congress recognized bourbon as a "distinctive product of the United States" on May 4, 1964, creating the Federal Standards of Identity for Bourbon and setting strict federal regulations that stipulate how bourbon is made. When you cook with bourbon, you're adding a distinct taste of America to your dish.

What is bourbon?

Today, bourbon whiskey is the only original spirit from this country. In the world of distilled spirits, there are two basic kinds – the alcohol produced by distilling fermented fruit drinks such as wine and cider, and the distilled spirits of beverages like beer that are made from fermenting grain or other plants. Generally, when wine is distilled and aged, you end up with brandy, or what used to be called brandywine; when beer is distilled and aged, you generally end up with whiskey. In essence then, whiskey is brandy made from beer instead of wine, and it developed in colder European countries where grapes couldn't thrive.

Geographically speaking, it could be said that there are four different kinds of whiskey out there: Irish whiskey, Scotch whisky, Canadian whisky, and American whiskey. Although countries such as India, Japan, and Russia have been trying their hand at whiskey production, they are relative newcomers on the scene and their inspiration comes from the Anglo-Saxon tradition. Of the different varieties of American whiskey, bourbon is, without a doubt, the most highly regarded.

All bourbon is therefore whiskey, but not all whiskey is bourbon. Specific standards require that bourbon whiskey: 1) consist of at least 51% corn, 2) be distilled at no more than 160 proof, 3) add nothing except distilled water, 4) be aged in new charred oak barrels, 5) be aged at least 2 years to be labeled as "straight bourbon whiskey," and 6) be produced in the U.S.

mention strong bones in its renowned thoroughbreds. The fermented product, known as "beer," is distilled to produce a clear spirit with an alcohol percent as high as 70, or 140 proof.

The result is a very strong liquor that often gets a subsequent dash of water before going into charred white oak barrels to age. This step is the most crucial in the production of bourbon, because the whiskey seeps into the barrel walls as they expand in the hot months and leeches back out during cooler weather as the wood contracts. As a result, color and flavor from the burnt wood on the surface and from the toasted wood underneath impart their unique characteristics on the bourbon. Predominant flavors in bourbon whiskey can be directly attributed to the qualities of the wood used for aging. Tastes such as those of the oak itself, the vanilla produced by the heated wood, and the sweet notes derived from caramelized wood sugars all lend bourbon its one-of-a-kind character and subtlety. After at least two years in the barrel, the aged whiskey can be labeled as bourbon.

Over time, some alcohol tends to evaporate through pores in the wood, so distillers often add water to the whiskey before bottling to achieve the desired proof. Barrel-proof bourbons have been bottled straight from the barrel, with no added water. The final product is a whiskey with a distinctive amber or honey-hued sheen and complex flavors and aromas reminiscent of molasses, caramel, vanilla, pecans, cinnamon, brown sugar, and a host of other culinary inspirations. For this reason, bourbon has long been a popular cooking ingredient, especially in the South.

How is bourbon made?

One of the legal requirements for bourbon is that it start with a mash consisting of at least 51 percent corn. The addition of rye, wheat and malted barley usually completes the blend and determines the final flavor profile of the whiskey. To make a sour mash, craftsmen crush the grains and combine them with water, and – much like with a sourdough starter for bread – mash from a previous batch is added to the mix. Aside from ensuring consistency, this process discourages the growth of wild yeast and bacteria that might affect the quality of the final product.

Also integral to the mix is good water. Aquifers and springs throughout Kentucky provide water exceptionally rich in limestone, something that facilitates good fermentation, not to

Appetizers

Sour Mash Pancakes
* with Smoked Trout Salad*
Vegetable Fritters
Buttermilk Dumplings with
* Roasted Red Pepper Sauce*
Red Shutter Meatballs
Pimento Cheese Toasts
Shrimp and Corn Hushpuppies
Plum Tomatoes with
* Goat Cheese and Prosciutto*
Sweet Potato and
* Goat Cheese Omelet*
Bourbon Benedictine
Hot Brown Tart

Unless otherwise stated, all recipes are
designed to feed 6-8 people.

Sour Mash Pancakes
with Smoked Trout Salad

Distiller's flour, the ground grains from the dried sour mash used in bourbon production, makes the perfect base for wholesome breads and baked goods with a hearty, distinctive flavor. Early farmers and distillers in Kentucky more often than not fed these flavorful and nutritious leftovers to livestock, but spent grains have been used by thrifty bakers in Europe for generations. This blini-inspired recipe pairs up the sweetness of distiller's flour with the richness of smoked trout for a great cocktail snack or the start to an elegant meal. If you can't get your hands on distiller's flour, several varieties of sour mash bread mixes are available online or at gift shops throughout the state.

2 cups distiller's flour
1 teaspoon baking powder
2 tablespoons sugar
1 teaspoon salt
¼ teaspoon freshly grated nutmeg
2 eggs, slightly beaten
1 cup buttermilk
2 tablespoons bourbon
2 tablespoons melted butter
Vegetable oil for frying
1 cup flaked smoked trout
¼ cup finely chopped green apple
2 tablespoons mayonnaise

Combine all of the dry ingredients in a large bowl. Mix together the eggs, buttermilk, and bourbon and add to the flour mixture, stirring just until the dry ingredients are moistened. Add the melted butter and mix until incorporated. Drop by tablespoons onto a hot greased griddle or skillet and fry, turning once, until browned on both sides. Serve warm with a spoonful of salad made by mixing together the flaked trout, green apple and mayonnaise. For a special treat, top off with a bit of caviar.

Sour Mash Bourbon Bread Company

When they were at the helm of Louisville's famous Oak-room in the Seelbach Hotel, Jim Gerhardt, Mike Cunha and Adam Seger came up with the idea for a signature sourdough bread with a subtle bourbon nuance to serve at the restaurant. Drawing on a distinctive distiller's blend of corn, rye and malted barley, the hearty bread quickly earned rave reviews, among them accolades from Julia Child, who proclaimed it "a delightful pick me up." Today, baking enthusiasts and bourbon aficionados can obtain a variety of mixes utilizing flavorful distiller's flour from the company they founded.

Sour Mash Bourbon Bread Company LLC
10001 Forest Green Blvd.
Louisville, Kentucky 40223
or go online at: www.atasteofkentucky.com

Schuckman's Fish Co. & Smokery

Lewis Shuckman, a third-generation fishmonger who operates the family business at his Louisville smokery, uses Pappy Van Winkle to impart exceptional flavor in his award-winning bourbon-style smoked trout. His smoked spoonfish, another regional specialty, has also gained national recognition for its exceptional quality. The spoonfish, also known as the paddlefish or spoonbill catfish, is one of the tastiest byproducts of recent trends in which Kentucky tobacco farmers have turned to aquaculture as a way of diversification. This relative of the sturgeon has firm, white flesh that has become a favorite with seafood aficionados across the country. Not only that, Kentucky spoonfish caviar such as that produced at Schuckman's Fish Co. & Smokery has received attention around the world for its exceptional quality.

Old Rip Van Winkle – A Topnotch Bourbon

The Old Rip Van Winkle Distillery boasts what many consider the highest rated whiskeys in the world. In a blind taste test of whiskeys from around the globe, The Beverage Tasting Institute in Chicago gave 20-year old Pappy Van Winkle's Family Reserve 99 out of 100 points, the highest score ever awarded. The 15-year old Pappy Van Winkle Family Reserve and Van Winkle's Special Reserve 12-Year Old have each received a 98 rating, higher than any other bourbon whiskeys. In addition, the 12-Year Old Special Reserve received the Trophy for Worldwide Whisky and a Best-In-Class Gold Medallion in the International Wine and Spirit Competition of 2008. With these awards under its belt, the Old Rip Van Winkle Distillery easily lays claim to being one of the best producers of bourbon in the world.

Much of the success of the Old Rip Van Winkle Distill-ery can be attributed to a history that covers four generations. The Van Winkle family involvement with bourbon began in the late 1800s with Julian P. "Pappy" Van Winkle, Sr., a traveling salesman for the W.L. Weller and Sons wholesale house in Louisville. Pappy and Alex Farnsley eventually bought the wholesale house and also purchased the A. Ph. Stitzel Distillery, which made bourbon for Weller. The two companies merged and became the Stitzel-Weller Distillery, with prominent brands such as W.L. Weller, Old Fitzgerald, Rebel Yell, and Cabin Still.

Pappy would have an influence there for many years and after his death, Julian, Jr. – his son – took over operations until stockholders forced the sale of the distillery in 1972. The rights to all but one of their brands were sold with the distillery or to other distilleries. That brand was Old Rip Van Winkle.

Julian, Jr. resurrected this pre-Prohibition label and used stores from the old distillery to supply his brand, and in 1981, his son, Julian, III, assumed control when he passed away. Since then, Julian, III has continued with the Van Winkle tradition of high-quality wheated bourbon. His son, Preston, came on board in 2001 and the Van Winkles plan on keeping their bourbon legacy alive for generations to come.

The Van Winkles entered into a joint venture with the Buffalo Trace Distillery, where their whiskey production takes place now. Each barrel foregoes the use of rye, a less expensive grain favored by many distillers, and opts for wheat instead. This lends the bourbon a mellow, sweet taste, which is enhanced by the extra aging the barrels receive in the warehouse.

We find that bourbons made with wheat age more gracefully than other bourbons made with rye.
Master Distiller Julian Van Winkle, III

2 cups canola oil for frying
2 cups all-purpose flour
1½ teaspoons baking powder
1 scant teaspoon kosher salt
½ teaspoon ground white pepper
½ teaspoon ground turmeric
1 large egg
1 cup buttermilk
4 tablespoons bourbon
½ cup grated zucchini
½ cup grated yellow squash
½ cup cooked baby lima beans
½ cup fresh corn kernels
½ cup fresh peas
½ cup diced, cooked carrots
½ cup sliced green onion

Vegetable Fritters

When summer has reached its climax, gardeners can expect a steady supply of fresh corn, tender peas, carrots, onion, baby limas and succulent zucchini and yellow squash. They figure prominently in this recipe for crispy fritters seasoned with the complementary flavors of bourbon and turmeric. Given the pungent, smoke-laden aromas of bitter orange and ginger that characterize turmeric, the exotic Asian spice derived from the root of the leafy *Curcuma longa* plant, an equally complex bourbon works well in this preparation. Because of the balanced notes of smoky wood and nutmeg that bring out the best in the vegetables, I like to use Elijah Craig Kentucky Straight Bourbon Whiskey. It's made by Parker Beam, Jim Beam's grandnephew, at Heaven Hill Distillery in Bardstown.

Heat the oil in a large cast-iron skillet over medium heat. Sift together the flour, baking powder, salt, pepper and turmeric in a large bowl. Whisk together the egg, buttermilk and bourbon and add to the dry ingredients, mixing until incorporated. Stir in the vegetables and mix well. Once the oil is hot enough that a bit of the batter dropped into it starts to sizzle, drop quarter-cup-sized portions of the mixture into the hot oil and fry till golden on one side, about 2-3 minutes. Turn over and fry the other side. Remove to a plate lined with a paper towel and drain to remove excess oil. Serve warm.

Buttermilk Dumplings with Roasted Red Pepper Sauce

Hearty and filling, dumplings are one of those dishes associated with comfort food and home cooking in this country. But, the humble dumpling can take many forms and have many flavors, including this light and fluffy variety with the zing of buttermilk. Paired with sweet notes of bourbon in the red pepper sauce, it makes for an elegant and tangy start to almost any meal.

2 cups fire-roasted sweet red peppers, with liquid
½ cup bourbon
½ cup heavy cream
Kosher salt
Ground white pepper
Smoked paprika
2 cups sifted all-purpose flour
½ teaspoon kosher salt
1 teaspoon baking powder
1 large egg, beaten
¾ cup buttermilk
¼ cup bourbon
Fresh snipped chives for garnish

To prepare the sauce, purée the red peppers with the bourbon and cream in a blender until perfectly smooth. Pour into a heavy saucepan over medium heat and cook, stirring often, for 15 minutes or until the sauce has thickened and reduced by half. Season with salt, pepper, and paprika as needed. While the sauce cooks, bring 2 quarts of salted water to a rolling boil and prepare the dumplings by mixing together the flour, salt, baking powder, egg, buttermilk and bourbon. Drop tablespoon-sized portions of the batter into the boiling water and cook for several minutes after the dumplings have floated to the surface. Use a slotted spoon to remove dumplings from the cooking liquid and keep warm in a covered bowl. To serve, ladle ½ cup of the sauce onto a soup plate and top with several dumplings. Garnish with fresh chives and enjoy.

Red Shutter Meatballs

Meatballs – one of the quintessential party foods. Perfect at a potluck for fifty or at a cocktail get-together for a dozen friends, meatballs are usually a big hit no matter what the flavor. Kicked up a bit with a healthy dose of fresh garlic and a generous splash of bourbon in the tangy sauce, this version is sure to please. Maker's Mark bourbon works especially well in this recipe, named for the iconic red shutters on the buildings at the picturesque distillery in Loretto, Kentucky.

1 pound ground beef
1 pound ground turkey
½ cup fresh bread crumbs
1 large egg, beaten
1 teaspoon kosher salt
1 tablespoon minced garlic
½ teaspoon dried thyme
½ ground black pepper
¼ teaspoon ground nutmeg
1 teaspoon hot sauce
2 tablespoons bourbon
1 tablespoon Worcestershire sauce
2 tablespoons olive oil
½ cup bourbon
½ cup sorghum
3 tablespoons hot sauce
½ cup firmly packed brown sugar
¾ cup apple cider vinegar
¼ cup tomato paste
½ teaspoon kosher salt
1 teaspoon smoked paprika

To make the meatballs, mix together the ground beef, turkey, bread crumbs, egg, salt, garlic, thyme, pepper, nutmeg, hot sauce, 2 tablespoons bourbon, and Worcestershire in a large bowl. Shape into meatballs of 1½-inch diameter. In a heavy skillet over a medium heat, brown meatballs in 2 tablespoons olive oil. Remove from pan and set aside. Drain off the excess grease and make the sauce in the same pan by adding the remaining ingredients to the pan and cooking over low heat for 5 minutes. Add meatballs to the sauce and coat thoroughly. Simmer, uncovered, for 30 minutes.

The Kentucky Bourbon Trail: Maker's Mark Distillery

The distinctive red-shuttered, black distillery buildings at Maker's Mark in Loretto were listed on the National Register of Historic Places in December of 1974, and four years later became a National Historic Landmark. Originally built as Burks' Distillery in 1889, it claims to be the first in the country to actively use landmark buildings for distilling. The current recipe for Maker's Mark was developed in 1951 and since then it has developed a cult following among some whiskey enthusiasts. For years it was marketed with the tag line, "It tastes expensive ... and is."

Bottled at 90 proof and sold in squarish bottles with a trade-marked red wax seal since 1958, Maker's Mark got its name from Margorie Samuels, the wife of founder Bill Samuels. Apart from coming up with the idea for the distinctive wax dipping with the dripping tendrils, she also designed the label with the star that represents Star Hill Farm, the land the distillery calls home.

For information about tours
of the distillery, contact:
Visitors Center at Maker's Mark Distillery
3350 Burks Spring Road
Loretto, Kentucky 40037
(270) 865-2099

Whisky or Whiskey?

Today, the spelling "whisky" is generally reserved for whiskies distilled in Scotland and Canada, whereas "whiskey" normally refers to spirits distilled in Ireland and the United States. According to a directive issued by the Bureau of Alcohol, Tobacco and Firearms in 1968, "whisky" is actually the official spelling in this country as well, however it permits the use of "whiskey" for labels in deference to American tradition. Even though most U.S. producers still use the spelling with the "e" there are exceptions – usually indicative of Scottish heritage – such as Early Times, Maker's Mark, and George Dickel. At one time, however, everyone spelled whisky without the "e." The addition of the "e" reportedly took place in the 1800s when Scottish distilleries began flooding the market with cheaper spirits produced using the Coffey still. To distinguish their higher quality product from their Scotch counterparts, Irish and American distilleries adopted an extra "e" in the spelling.

1 pound each yellow and
  white extra-sharp
  Cheddar cheese
2 tablespoons bourbon
1¼ cups mayonnaise
1½ cups roasted red peppers,
  finely diced
½ teaspoon kosher salt
½ teaspoon ground
  white pepper
10-12 slices whole
  wheat bread
Vegetable oil spray
Green onion for garnish

Pimento Cheese Toasts

Pimento cheese is said to be one of those quintessential southern comfort foods, but I have fond memories of growing up in Wisconsin on this savory mixture of shredded cheese, chopped pimentos and mayonnaise. Coming from a state known for its dairy products, I guess it's hardly surprising that any recipe with cheese in it would eventually make its way there – if it didn't originate there in the first place. This recipe calls for a generous dose of Old Forester, the official bourbon of Louisville, something that ensures its Bluegrass lineage.

Start by grating the cheeses. Then, purée the white Cheddar with the bourbon and half the mayonnaise in a food processor to form a smooth paste. Spoon into a mixing bowl with the remaining mayonnaise and add the yellow cheese, diced red peppers, salt and pepper and combine. Refrigerate for at least two hours to allow the flavors to meld and the cheese to set up. To assemble the cheese toasts, cut the bread slices in half diagonally and pinch together the two farthest corners of each triangular slice to form little horns. If the bread is not soft enough that a good pinch seals it together, you may want to use a toothpick to keep each horn together. Lay the cornucopia out on a baking sheet, spray with a bit of vegetable oil and pop into a 375-degree oven for 5 minutes or until the toasts have browned somewhat. Remove from the oven and immediately fill each horn with 1-2 tablespoons of pimento cheese and serve warm with a garnish of green onion.

Shrimp and Corn Hushpuppies

Although they are now available in many areas of the country on the menus at fast-food seafood restaurants, hushpuppies are one of those distinctly southern foods. The name "hushpuppies" reportedly arose when early hunters or pioneers would quickly fry cornmeal and feed it to the dogs to "hush the puppies" around the cookfires. Most often served alongside fried fish and seafood, they can make a wonderful snack or appetizer on their own – especially when you add sweet corn and chunks of juicy shrimp.

2 cups finely ground cornmeal
6 tablespoons all-purpose flour
4 tablespoons granulated sugar
2 teaspoons kosher salt
1 teaspoon ground white pepper
½ cup water
½ cup bourbon
½ cup buttermilk
1½ teaspoons baking powder
2 small eggs, lightly beaten
2 cups raw shrimp, shelled, deveined and chopped
1 cup frozen corn kernels, thawed
¼ cup chopped green onion
Canola oil, sufficient for deep-frying

Mix together cornmeal, flour, sugar, salt, and pepper. Bring water and bourbon to a roiling boil and add the cornmeal mixture, combining until moistened. Remove from the heat and let cool for 10 minutes. Add buttermilk, baking powder, eggs, shrimp, corn kernels and onion. Mix well. Fill a heavy pan with 3 inches of oil and heat to 375 degrees. Carefully drop full teaspoons of dough into hot oil and fry about 1 minute on each side, or until golden brown and cooked

through. Drain on paper towels, sprinkle with a bit of kosher salt and serve hot. Early Times, an affordable bourbon from Louisville, works well in this recipe.

21

8-10 medium plum tomatoes
12 ounces soft goat cheese
½ cup prosciutto, roughly chopped
2 tablespoons bourbon
2 tablespoons fresh bread crumbs,
  plus extra for the top
¼ teaspoon kosher salt
Cracked black pepper
Fresh chives for garnish

Halve the tomatoes with a sharp paring knife and remove the seeds and pulp and set aside. (If desired, use a zig-zag cut to give the tomatoes a festive look.) Combine the goat cheese, prosciutto, bourbon, bread crumbs, and salt in a bowl. Spoon a tablespoon of the mixture into each tomato half, sprinkle with cracked pepper and bread crumbs and place in a baking dish under a boiler for 5 minutes or until the cheese has started to brown. Remove from the oven and serve immediately with a garnish of fresh chives and toasted white bread.

Photo by James Asher

Plum Tomatoes with Goat Cheese and Prosciutto

Tomatoes and bourbon? Most people wouldn't think it, but the natural sweetness in Kentucky whiskey works as a wonderful enhancer to the earthy goodness of ripe plum tomatoes. Filled with tangy goat cheese with chunks of prosciutto, a plate of these makes a satisfying summer lunch or early fall brunch.

Sweet Potato and Goat Cheese Omelet

Although omelets are a wonderful morning dish, they make the perfect light lunch or an elegant first course for a special evening meal. Legend has it that when Napoleon Bonaparte was traveling through the south of France with his army, he spent the night near Bessières, a town known for its delicious egg dishes. He enjoyed an omelet prepared by a local innkeeper so much that he ordered the villagers to gather all the available eggs, and the next day they prepared an enormous omelet for the whole army. This recipe won't feed an entire army, but it will provide a tasty bite to whet an appetite before a hearty fall supper. Served alongside a helping of cucumber spears and watercress or with a bowl of asparagus bisque, it makes a simple, yet classy, summer dinner. A nice barrel-proof bourbon like Wild Turkey Rare Breed works well here.

For each omelet:

1 teaspoon butter
1 teaspoon olive oil
2 large eggs, at room temperature
1½ teaspoons bourbon
1½ teaspoons heavy cream
¼ teaspoon kosher salt
¼ teaspoon ground black pepper
1 small sweet potato, cooked and sliced
2 ounces goat cheese

Melt the butter in the olive oil in a heavy skillet over medium-low heat. Whisk together the eggs, bourbon and cream until the eggs are pale yellow and frothy. Stir in the salt and pepper and pour the mixture into the skillet once the butter has melted completely and has started to sizzle. Once the eggs have started to firm up, lay the sweet potato slices in a row down the center of the omelet and top with the goat cheese. After the cheese starts to melt a bit, fold over and serve with a garnish of chopped fresh tomato and micro basil.

Bourbon Benedictine

One of the most famous figures to emerge from Kentucky kitchens was Miss Jennie Benedict, a Louisville caterer who opened a downtown restaurant in the 1890s. Known for her wonderful cakes and tea sandwiches, she concocted a special cream cheese-and-cucumber spread that still lives on today. Although it's most often used as a filling for sandwiches, it also makes a great dip for vegetables and crackers.

1 large English cucumber, coarsely chopped
2 tablespoons chopped white onion
¼ cup chopped fresh parsley
¼ cup bourbon (I like to use Four Roses.)
¼ cup mayonnaise
16 ounces cream cheese, softened
1 teaspoon kosher salt
½ teaspoon ground white pepper

In a food processor, purée the cucumber, skin and all, with the onion. Remove from the processor and use a clean towel or a bit of cheesecloth to squeeze all the liquid out of the mixture that you can. Set aside. Return to the food processor and purée the parsley with the bourbon and mayonnaise to form a smooth paste. This will give the Benedictine its characteristically green color without using food coloring. Add the cream cheese to the processor and pulse until smooth. Transfer to the bowl with the onion-cucumber mix, season with the salt and pepper, and combine thoroughly. Refrigerate for at least an hour and enjoy with celery and pretzel sticks.

To make finger sandwiches, spread 2–3 tablespoons of the benedictine on a slice of pumpernickel bread, top with another slice, and press firmly together. Chill for at least an hour. Use a serrated knife to remove the crusts and cut lengthwise into 3 or 4 small sandwiches. Spread one side with a bit of mayonnaise and dip into chopped parsley for an attractive presentation.

Hot Brown Tart

No trip to Louisville, Kentucky would be complete without a trip to the famous Brown Hotel to sample the local culinary legend known as the Hot Brown. This landmark sandwich came about in 1926 when Chef Fred K. Schmidt constructed a decadent open-faced turkey sandwich topped with Mornay sauce and bacon to satisfy the appetites of late-night dancers in downtown Louisville. Today, it's a staple in most Kentucky kitchens with many spin-offs, including this savory tart that is perfect for brunches and late-night suppers. The sweet notes of Jim Beam add a distinct flavor to this quiche-inspired dish.

Pastry dough for a 12-inch cast-iron skillet
6 large eggs
1 cup heavy cream
¼ cup bourbon
½ teaspoon kosher salt
½ teaspoon ground white pepper
1 cup chopped cooked turkey breast
1 cup grated white,
    extra-sharp Cheddar cheese
8 slices cooked (not too crispy) bacon,
    chopped
2 small tomatoes, thinly sliced
¼ cup grated Parmesan cheese

Preheat the oven to 375 degrees and line the skillet with the pastry dough. Beat the eggs with the cream, bourbon, salt, and pepper. Place turkey breast on tart crust, and top with the Cheddar cheese and bacon. Pour the egg mixture over the cheese, and layer tomatoes over the top. Sprinkle with the Parmesan cheese and bake for 30 minutes or until a knife inserted in the middle comes out clean. The top should be brown and crusty. Remove from the oven, let sit for 5 minutes and serve piping hot.

The Kentucky Bourbon Trail: Jim Beam Distillery

In more than two centuries of existence, not a single day has passed without a Beam family member acting as master distiller in what many consider one of the greatest business dynasties in American history. It all started in the late 1700s when large numbers of Germans began arriving in this country. One of these imigrants, Johannes "Jacob" Boehm, would settle in the lush bluegrass hills of Kentucky to try his hand at farming, eventually changing the spelling of his last name to Beam. Like many farmers of the day, Beam also knew the art of distilling and he sold his first barrels of corn whiskey around 1795. It was known as Old Jake Beam.

In 1820, Beam's eighteen-year-old son, David, took over and expanded the family's bourbon business during a time of industrial revolution. His son, David M. Beam, moved the distillery to Nelson County in 1854 to capitalize on the growing network of rail lines, and in 1933 the distillery was rebuilt in Clermont by Colonel James B. Beam. It was the Colonel who managed the business before and after Prohibition, and it was during this time that the bourbon was renamed in his honor. Today, master distiller Fred Noe carries on the tradition at one of the most famous distilleries in the world.

Free tours of Jim Beam are offered year round.
For more information, contact:
Jim Beam
526 Happy Hollow Rd.
Clermont, Kentucky 40110
(502) 543-9877

Master Distiller Fred Noe says:

Bourbon can add a lot to ordinary recipes, and it can enhance food in two ways. If you enjoy a nice bourbon with your meal, the finish of the bourbon will carry over to the food that is being eaten. If the foods are prepared with bourbon in the recipe, then the flavor is in the food being consumed. I enjoy both – drinking the bourbon with food and enjoying foods prepared with bourbon.

I enjoy tasting foods that have been prepared with bourbon and I think bourbon should be used in recipes when it makes the dish better. Good cooks know how to use bourbon to create unique foods drawing on the flavors in good bourbons. There are lighter bourbons that can be used for salad dressings and sauces for fish and poultry, and heavier bourbons can bring a big bold flavor to the dish. I like to see cooks implement bourbon to add flavor from the aging in the white oak barrels and sweetness from the corn.

My father started a tradition in our family that is a great way to enhance the flavor of pork chops on the grill. After grilling nice, thick

chops, place them on a platter and flambé with Booker's Bourbon. For the flambé, sprinkle bourbon on the chops and light to burn off the alcohol. To see how much flavor this adds, do a taste test and compare chops that have been flambéed with those that have not.

The Beam family has always enjoyed cooking with bourbon almost as much as drinking it. My father, Booker Noe, enjoyed seeing what flavors he could enhance with the addition of a little bourbon. For example, I once saw him add bourbon to his malted milk shake during a stop at the Dairy Dip after one of our fishing trips. I think he looked forward to the malts more than me.

Soups

Unless otherwise stated, all recipes are designed for 6-8 people.

Cream of Cauliflower

With its pale honey sheen, Four Roses has both a light body and flavor with sweet notes of citrus and vanilla. Here it provides a slightly spicy backdrop for the earthy taste of cauliflower and onion.

1 medium yellow onion, chopped
½ cup chopped celery
2 large cloves garlic, minced
2 tablespoons olive oil
1 medium potato, peeled and diced
1 large head cauliflower, chopped or
  broken into florets (about 2½ pounds)
1 cup bourbon
4 cups chicken stock
2½ teaspoons kosher salt
½ teaspoon ground white pepper
¼ teaspoon freshly grated nutmeg
¼ teaspoon turmeric
2 cups half-and-half
Dried thyme

In a large kettle over medium-high heat, sweat the onion, celery, and garlic in the olive oil; add the potato and cauliflower and continue cooking for 5 minutes. Pour in the bourbon, cover and let steam for another 5 minutes. Add the stock, salt, pepper, nutmeg and turmeric and bring to a boil. Reduce the heat to low and simmer, covered, for 30 minutes or until cauliflower and potatoes are fork tender. Use a stick blender to purée the potato-and-cauliflower mixture in the cooking liquid to the desired consistency. Stir in the half-and-half, warm through and correct the seasoning before serving. Sprinkle with the dried thyme.

The Kentucky Bourbon Trail: The Four Roses Story

According to legend, it started when Four Roses founder Paul Jones, Jr. became enamored of a southern belle. He sent the beauty a proposal of marriage, and she promised to wear a corsage of roses on her gown to the upcoming grand ball if she accepted. Paul Jones waited with bated breath that night, thrilled to see his sweetheart finally arrive with a corsage of four red roses. As a symbol of his devotion, Jones would eventually use a floral logo in the whiskey he produced, and this passion would become evident in Four Roses Bourbon.

Today, Four Roses claims to be the only distillery that combines five proprietary yeast strains with two separate mash-bills to produce ten distinct bourbon recipes, each with its own unique character and rich, fruity flavors. All of these recipes age in new white oak barrels in one-of-a-kind single-story rack warehouses, and are married together to create Four Roses Yellow. Four come together to produce Four Roses Small Batch Bourbon, and one will be hand-selected for Four Roses Single Barrel Bourbon. Once in a while, the master distiller will select an exceptional single barrel, or marry a small number of recipes to create the highly acclaimed limited release Four Roses Bourbon.

Built in 1910 with unique Spanish Mission-Style architecture, the Four Roses Distillery is nestled on the banks of the Salt River in the quiet countryside near Lawrenceburg.

For more information, contact:
Four Roses Distillery
1224 Bonds Mill Road
Lawrenceburg, Kentucky 40342
(502) 839-3436

Photo from Four Roses Distillery

Why Kentucky?

According to most statistics, more than 95% of the world's bourbon is made in Kentucky. Why is that? After Daniel Boone discovered the pass at the Cumberland Gap in the 1700s, pioneers made their way through the Appalachians and settled the virgin land that would become Kentucky. Many brought their families to the central part of the region in the 1780s and there they established frontier towns such as Bardstown and Frankfort; others made their way to the falls of the Ohio and founded the river city of Louisville. Many of these early settlers had their ancestry in Scotland and Ireland – both countries with strong distilling traditions – and with them they brought whiskey-making skills passed down from one generation to the next.

A hardy native crop, corn thrived in Kentucky, and farmer-distillers soon found a use for surplus corn in a new kind of whiskey. Purified water, an essential ingredient in making whiskey, was abundant in the many local springs from underground limestone beds. This combination, along with an ideal climate, yielded whiskey with a unique smoothness and sweeter flavor that only mellowed and increased in popularity after aging in the oak barrels used for shipping. Soon, this sought-after whiskey would set the standard, and bourbon would become synonymous with fine Kentucky whiskey.

Photo by James Asher

Potato and Leek Purée with Smoked Salmon

This creamy soup features Knob Creek Bourbon, a small batch selection from Jim Beam with bright aromas of rye and sea salt that highlight the caper garnish. The spicy, somewhat biting palate of the bourbon pairs well with the bit of horseradish in the soup, and the Knob Creek finish – slightly oily, yet smooth and long – makes it a perfect match for the richness of the smoked salmon. Enjoy this soup with a dash of fresh lemon juice and serve with a green salad and toasted pumpernickel.

2 tablespoons olive oil
2 tablespoons unsalted butter
2 large leeks, cleaned and chopped
  (about 3 cups)
6 cloves garlic, smashed
4 pounds red potatoes, peeled and diced
1 sprig fresh thyme
2 cups bourbon
10 cups chicken stock
3 teaspoons kosher salt
½ teaspoon ground white pepper
2 teaspoons prepared horseradish
½ teaspoon freshly grated nutmeg
1 cup heavy cream
12 ounces sliced smoked salmon
Capers for garnish

In a large stockpot heat the olive oil and butter over medium heat and sauté the leeks, onion and garlic until soft. Add the diced potatoes, thyme and bourbon and simmer until half of the bourbon has cooked off. Add the chicken stock, salt, pepper, horseradish, and nutmeg and cook, uncovered, until the potatoes are soft, approximately 30 minutes. To finish the soup, add the cream and purée using a hand blender. Add half of the smoked salmon, which has been roughly chopped, and heat through. Add additional salt, pepper, and horseradish to taste. Ladle the potato-leek purée into bowls and garnish with bits of remaining smoked salmon and capers.

Corn and Sweet Potato Chowder

Bottled at 90 proof and aged for ten years, Eagle Rare Single Barrel is a Kentucky straight bourbon based on a rye recipe. With its colors of topaz and polished bronze, it has early aromas of buttered toast and young tobacco. The palate shows sweet flavors of raisins and almonds. Its long finish, redolent of corn and moderately fiery, make it the perfect addition to this hearty soup.

2 tablespoons butter
3 tablespoons olive oil
2 large yellow onions, coarsely chopped
4-5 large cloves garlic, minced
2 teaspoons kosher salt
½ teaspoon ground cumin
½ teaspoon ground white pepper
½ ground black pepper
½ teaspoon dried thyme
4 tablespoons all-purpose flour
1 cup bourbon
6 cups whole milk
2 large sweet potatoes,
   peeled and cut in large chunks
3 cups fresh corn kernels
3 tablespoons all-purpose flour
½ cup heavy cream
Fresh cilantro for garnish

Melt the butter with the olive oil over medium heat in a heavy-bottomed soup pot. Add the onions, garlic, salt, cumin, and pepper, and cook for 5 minutes, stirring frequently. Whisk in the 4 tablespoons of flour and stir for 30 seconds. Slowly add the bourbon, whisking constantly to prevent lumps from forming. When the mixture starts to boil, add the milk and sweet potatoes. Simmer, uncovered, over low heat, stirring often, until the sweet potatoes are tender, about 30 minutes. Add the corn kernels and simmer another 5 minutes, seasoning with additional salt and pepper as needed. To thicken the chowder, whisk together the 3 tablespoons of flour and cream and stir into the soup. Warm through, adjust the seasoning and ladle into individual soup bowls to enjoy. Garnish with sprigs of fresh cilantro or kernels of corn.

16 ounces dried lentils (about 2 cups)
16 ounces country sausage
6 cups low-sodium chicken stock
1 cup bourbon
1 very large yellow onion,
    coarsely chopped (about 2 cups)
1 large red bell pepper, diced
    (about 1 cup)
2 large bay leaves
2 teaspoons kosher salt
1 teaspoon ground black pepper
1 teaspoon smoked paprika
½ teaspoon dried oregano
½ teaspoon dried thyme
2 tablespoons apple cider vinegar
2 tablespoons hot sauce

Lentils and Country Sausage

Lentil plants originated in the Near East and have been part of the human diet since Neolithic times. They come in large and small sizes, and their colors can range from yellow, or orange and red to green, brown and black. At 26%, lentils have one of the highest levels of protein of any plant-based food. For this recipe, I like to use Virginia Gentleman – a bourbon not produced in Kentucky – but almost any will do.

Rinse the lentils under cold running water. Transfer to a bowl, cover with lukewarm water, and let soak for two hours. In a large skillet, fry large chunks of the sausage over a medium heat until deep brown and crispy on the outside. Remove the pieces to a plate lined with a paper towel to remove any excess grease. Once the lentils have soaked, drain and transfer to a large soup pot or Dutch oven. Add the chicken stock, bourbon, onion, red pepper, bay leaves, salt and spices. Add the country sausage pieces and cook over medium heat for 45 minutes, or until the lentils have become tender. Stir in the vinegar and hot sauce before correcting the seasoning and enjoy with large slices of crusty bread or garlic corn pone.

Virginia Gentleman

A bourbon producer outside of Kentucky? Yes, there is indeed such a thing. Although most of the country's bourbon distillers are located in Kentucky, there is no law requiring that bourbon be produced in the state. The A. Smith Bowman Distillery opened shortly after the end of Prohibition, when Virginia native Abram Bowman decided to boost profits from his cornfield by making whiskey. Aside from producing a variety of spirits such as vodka, scotch, tequila, rum, and gin, all under the namesake Bowman's brand, this Fredericksburg distillery has the Virginia Gentleman brand, a label that has developed something of a cult following over the years. In 1998 Bowman Distillery successfully launched Virginia Gentleman 90 Proof Small Batch Bourbon, a new premium bourbon that is the result of more than ten decades of family distilling tradition. The nose is slightly figgy with a bit of caramel and the taste shows delicate traits of apple and malt.

Bourbon Burgoo

This hearty soup hearkens back to early days when pioneers utilized huge cast-iron kettles and an abundance of local game to satisfy hungry crowds. Nowadays it's a traditional feature of many holiday celebrations in Kentucky, especially Derby Day in early May. Although traditional recipes often call for 24 hours of simmering, this updated, lighter version can be enjoyed in a fraction of the time. Since it's a traditionally rustic kind of dish, I like to use an equally rustic bourbon such as Cabin Still.

1 large red onion, diced
1 stalk celery, diced
4 cloves garlic, minced
1 small green bell pepper, diced
2 tablespoons olive oil
½ pound diced beef
½ pound diced pork
½ pound boneless chicken breast, diced
3 cups bourbon
4 cups chicken stock
4 cups beef stock
¼ cup Worcestershire sauce
2 large red potatoes, diced
2 large carrots, diced
½ cup lima beans
½ cup yellow corn
2 bay leaves
1 cup tomato paste
1 tablespoon kosher salt
Fresh ground black pepper
Chopped parsley for garnish

In a large Dutch oven, sauté the onion, celery, garlic and pepper in the olive oil over medium heat for 5 minutes. Add the beef, pork and chicken and brown for 10 minutes. Add the bourbon and stir to deglaze the bottom of the pan. Cook for 10 minutes, or until the liquid is reduced by half. Add stocks, Worcestershire sauce, vegetables, bay leaves and tomato paste and bring to a rolling boil. Reduce the heat and simmer, uncovered, for 2 hours. Add the salt and pepper to taste before serving. Garnish with the fresh chopped parsley.

Kentucky Gumbo

This hearty gumbo gets its distinctly Bluegrass flavor from the addition of chopped country ham and – what else? – a very generous dose of whiskey. For a special treat, splurge and get a bottle of Booker's for this dish. Dark orange with a rich, complex nose of plum and toasted pecans, and a long peppery finish, it's great both for cooking and sipping with gumbo. Woodford Reserve is another wonderful sipping bourbon with gumbo.

2 tablespoons olive oil
2 tablespoons unsalted butter
2 large bone-in chicken breasts with skin
  (2½ pounds total)
Kosher salt
Freshly ground black pepper
2 cups cubed country ham
2 cups sliced andouille sausage
2 celery ribs, with leaves, diced
1 large green bell pepper, diced
1 large red bell pepper, diced
1 medium red onion, diced
4 large cloves garlic, minced
⅓ cup all-purpose flour
2 cups bourbon
6 cups chicken broth
2 cups peeled, diced tomatoes
Cooked white long-grain rice
Thinly sliced green onion for garnish

In a heavy pot, heat the oil and butter until it smokes. Season the breasts with the salt and pepper and brown, skin side down, over high heat, about 5 minutes; turn over and cook until browned on the other side. Transfer to a plate and discard the skin. In the same pan, brown the country ham over medium heat and add to the plate with the chicken. Brown the sausage and add to the chicken and ham. Cook the celery, bell peppers, onion, and garlic over medium heat until lightly browned. Whisk in the flour, stirring constantly until the flour browns and smells nutty. Pour in the bourbon, stirring to make sure there are no lumps and cook for 10 minutes or until the bourbon has reduced by half. Add the broth and tomatoes; bring to a rolling boil. Reduce the heat to low and add the chicken, ham, and andouille. Cover and simmer until the chicken starts to fall from the bone, about 45 minutes. Remove the chicken, remove the bone and tear the chicken into pieces using a fork before returning to the soup. Serve with a spoon of the white rice and a scattering of the green onions.

Photo from Woodford Reserve Distillery

Shrimp and Bourbon Bisque

Alluring, spicy aromas of candied orange peel and dried citrus hint at the complex, powerful flavors in amber-red Blanton's bourbon. Somewhat sugary, somewhat spicy, this single-barrel delicacy enhances the buttery notes of this cream-based soup while bringing out the sweetness of the shrimp. I find that Evan Williams and Kentucky Tavern also work very well here.

3 pounds shrimp
2 tablespoons olive oil
2 teaspoons kosher salt
½ teaspoon ground white pepper
3 cups bourbon
4 tablespoons unsalted butter
1 large white onion, chopped
1 cup diced celery
1-2 cloves garlic, minced
2 tablespoons all-purpose flour
2 tablespoons tomato paste
6 cups chicken stock
½ teaspoon freshly grated nutmeg
2 cups heavy cream
3 tablespoons all-purpose flour
Freshly squeezed lemon juice
Whole shrimp for garnish (optional)

Coarsely chop the shrimp after peeling and deveining them; reserve the shells. Pour the olive oil into a heavy stockpot or a large Dutch oven over high heat and cook the shrimp just until opaque. Season with a bit of the salt and pepper, remove from the pan and set aside. Add the shrimp shells to the pan and cook, stirring occasionally, until shells turn brown. Add the bourbon to the shells and cook, stirring constantly, until the liquid reduces by half. Remove the shells, transfer the liquid to a bowl and set aside. Add the butter to the pan and melt over medium heat. Add the onion, celery and garlic and cook for 10 minutes or until the vegetables are soft. Add 2 tablespoons of flour and cook, stirring constantly, to incorporate and then add the tomato paste and cook another minute or two. Add the stock, nutmeg, remaining salt and pepper, and bring to a simmer, uncovered, for 15 minutes. Purée the soup using a handheld blender and pour through a strainer to remove most of the solids. Discard the solids, and return the strained liquid to a pan set over a low heat. Add the shrimp liquid and chopped shrimp, and turn up the heat. When the soup starts to bubble, whisk the cream and 3 tablespoons of flour together and add to the soup to thicken. Add the lemon juice, salt and pepper to taste, and divide soup among 6 or 8 bowls. Garnish with celery leaves, or, if desired, whole shrimp floating on a crouton raft.

Country Ham and Potato Stew

Bourbon adds a sweet backdrop to this rustic potato soup studded with large chunks of country ham, a specialty in southern states such as Virginia, Kentucky and Tennessee. To stand up to the salt and minerals in the ham, try a big-boned bourbon such as W.L. Weller or the more expensive Eagle Rare.

3 tablespoons olive oil
1 large yellow onion, diced
3-4 cloves garlic, minced
4 tablespoons all-purpose flour
1 cup bourbon
6 cups chicken broth
2 cups whole milk
2 cups diced country ham
3 pounds red potatoes, peeled
　　and cut in 1-inch chunks
2 large bay leaves
½ teaspoon ground
　　white pepper
½ teaspoon freshly
　　grated nutmeg

Heat the olive oil in a large stockpot over low heat and sauté the onion and garlic until translucent. Add the flour and cook for 5 minutes, stirring constantly so the roux doesn't burn. Slowly pour in the bourbon and mix well. Add the broth and bring to a boil. Reduce the heat, add the remaining ingredients and simmer for approximately 30 minutes, or until the potatoes have become tender. Add salt and pepper to taste and enjoy with slices of homemade toast.

Bourbon Butternut Squash Soup

Wild Turkey recently came out with a delicious liquor sweetened with honey that makes the perfect compliment to the warm spices and savory butternut squash in this elegant soup. If you can't get your hands on Wild Turkey American Honey, mix two parts bourbon with one part clover honey for a good substitute.

namon, pepper and cumin. Pour in the broth and simmer, covered, for 25 minutes or until the pieces of squash have started to break down. Use a handheld blender to purée the soup in the saucepan until perfectly smooth. Correct the seasoning and enjoy with a drizzle of the pumpkin seed oil and a sprinkle of the smoked paprika.

1 medium yellow onion, diced
4-5 cloves garlic, smashed
4 tablespoons unsalted butter
3 pounds butternut squash, diced,
   peeled and deseeded (about 6-7 cups)
2 cups Wild Turkey American Honey
3 teaspoons kosher salt
½ teaspoon ground ginger
½ teaspoons nutmeg
½ teaspoon ground cinnamon
½ teaspoon ground white pepper
½ teaspoon cumin
5½ cups chicken broth
Pumpkin seed oil
Smoked paprika

Sauté the onions and garlic in the butter in a 4-quart saucepan over medium heat until the onions become transluscent. Add the squash and cook an additional 5 minutes. Turn up the heat and add the American Honey, cooking until the liquid has reduced by half. Stir in the salt, ginger, nutmeg, cin-

Bourbon Barrel Foods

Kentucky native Matt Jamie has come up with an innovative way to use the spent oak barrels after bourbon has aged. In 2006 he started Bourbon Barrel Foods, LLC and since then he has developed a steadily growing line of edible merchandise that "portrays the essence, mystic and style of Kentucky's bourbon country." Bourbon Barrel Aged Worcestershire Sauce, his first product, combines all-natural, vegetarian Bluegrass ingredients with the sweetness of pure sorghum, and today his product line continues to expand.

Charred barrel staves figure prominently in the subtle flavors that characterize the Bourbon Smoked Sea Salt, a natural salt harvested from the Pacific, and woody flavors define the Bourbon Smoked Paprika and the Bourbon Smoked Peppercorns. Jamie recently unveiled a new line of sorghums as well. Blueberry Sorghum, Kentucky Sweet Sorghum and Bourbon Vanilla Sorghum bottle the earthy goodness of "Kentucky's maple syrup," inspiring a variety of uses in both sweet and savory dishes.

Jamie has also started using Kentucky-grown soybeans to produce Bourbon Barrel Aged Soy Sauce, a meaty brew with undertones of charcoal and spice, which qualifies his as the only company in the country to make its own soy sauce from scratch with locally grown soybeans.

For more information on spices and condiments from Bourbon Barrel Foods, contact:
Bourbon Barrel Foods, LLC
1201 Story Avenue, Suite 175
Louisville, Kentucky 40206
(502) 333-6103

Asparagus Bisque

A good source of folic acid, potassium, dietary fiber, and rutin, delicate-flavored asparagus has been used since early days as both a vegetable and medicine. This comforting, yet elegant, soup draws on the alkaline properties of whiskey to bring out the umami characteristic of the asparagus. The warm notes of white pepper and orange peel present in Russell's Reserve, a small-batch, ten-year-old bourbon created by Jimmy Russell and his son Eddie, provide the ideal finish in this recipe, but you're sure to find that most any bourbon will do the trick.

2 tablespoons olive oil
2 tablespoons unsalted butter
2½ pounds fresh asparagus, cut into pieces
1 large yellow onion, roughly chopped
2 large shallots, chopped
6 large cloves garlic, peeled and smashed
1 cup bourbon
¼ cup chopped fresh parsley
4 cups chicken stock
4 large bay leaves
2 teaspoons kosher salt
3 cups half-and-half
3 heaping tablespoons all-purpose flour
1 teaspoon ground white pepper
¼ teaspoon freshly grated nutmeg

Heat the olive oil and butter in a large stock pot over a very high heat and sauté the asparagus, covered, with the onion, shallots, and garlic for 10 minutes or until the asparagus begins to brown. Add the bourbon and parsley and simmer until half of the liquid has evaporated. Add the chicken stock, bay leaves and salt to the pot. Bring to a boil, cover and simmer for 30 minutes or until all the asparagus pieces are tender. Once the asparagus has cooked, purée the mixture in a blender until it is very smooth. Strain the mixture through a sieve over a clean pot, removing the coarsest of the pulp, about half a cup. Turn the heat up to medium high and return the strained mixture to the pot. Combine the half-and-half with the flour and the leftover pulp that has been strained out and purée until perfectly smooth. Add the purée, pepper, and nutmeg to the pot and cook, whisking constantly, for 5 minutes. The soup should be thick enough to coat the back of a spoon. Correct the seasoning. Enjoy this elegant and satisfying soup on its own or as a starter to a special dinner.

Master Distiller Jimmy Russell

A fixture on Kentucky's bourbon scene for more than fifty years, James C. Russell is master distiller at the Wild Turkey Distillery in Lawrenceburg. Known by everyone as Jimmy, he has worked at the distillery since 1954 and comes from a long line of bourbon workers. Director of the Kentucky Distillers Association, Jimmy Russell has become a recognized representative for the local bourbon industry and can often be found traipsing the world as a goodwill ambassador for the Bluegrass State's most famous export. He nonetheless finds time to sneak away and lead frequent tours at the distillery that owes so much to his dedication and commitment to success.

Wild Turkey is put into the barrel at a lower (and more expensive) proof. It's like making a great soup; if you cook it longer at a lower temperature, you retain the best flavors.

Master Distiller Jimmy Russell

Associate Distiller Eddie Russell

As the fourth generation Russell to work at Wild Turkey, Jimmy's son, Edward Freeman Russell, has an enviable pedigree in the bourbon industry. He has worked at the Austin Nichols distillery for more than a quarter of a century and occupied the position as Manager of Barrel Maturation and Warehousing when he and his father developed award-winning Russell's Reserve. His recent promotion to associate distiller ensures an even closer collaboration for this father-son team and promises more good things to come for fans of Wild Turkey.

Chicken Broth with Brown Rice Dumplings

This recipes works especially well with an easy-drinking bourbon like Evan Williams. Widely considered "Kentucky's first distiller," Williams arrived in 1783 and set up a small distillery along the Ohio River at the foot of what is now Fifth Street in downtown Louisville. Heaven Hill Distilleries bottles the bourbon that bears his name today.

1 large, whole chicken
2 quarts water
2 cups bourbon
2 large yellow onions, cut in half
2 large carrots, cut in pieces
2 teaspoons kosher salt
2 cups cooked brown rice
1 cup fresh bread crumbs
¼ cup grated Parmesan cheese
3 tablespoons chopped flat-leaf parsley
1 medium egg, beaten
1 pinch freshly grated nutmeg

In a large stockpot over a medium heat, cook the chicken with the water, bourbon, onions, carrots and salt for an hour or until the meat starts to fall from the bone. Take the chicken and vegetables out of the pot and set aside. (These can be served by themselves later in the meal or the chicken meat can be used for soup or salad.) Strain the broth and let cool in the refrigerator. Once cooled, skim off the top layer of fat and return to the stove over medium heat. To make the dumplings, combine the rice, bread crumbs, cheese, parsley, egg and nutmeg in a small bowl. Once the broth has started to bubble at the edge of the pot, form small, golf ball-size dumplings with your hands and drop into the simmering broth. Cook for 10 or 15 minutes, correct the seasoning and enjoy.

Salads

Kentucky Derby Salad
Turnip Green Slaw
Dandelion Greens
  with Haricots Verts and
  New Red Potatoes
Baby Spinach
  with English Peas, Red Pepper
  and Roasted Garlic
Grilled Hearts of Romaine
  with Bleu Cheese and
  Black-Eyed Peas
Mâche with Sliced Potatoes and
  Sweet Corn Vinaigrette
Watercress and Cucumber Spears
  with Woodford Reserve
  Citrus Vinaigrette
Cold Brown Salad with
  Bourbon Buttermilk Dressing
Bibb Salad with Roasted Root Vegetables
  and Bourbon Molasses Vinaigrette
Green River Cabbage

Unless otherwise stated, all recipes are designed for 6-8 people.

Kentucky Derby Salad

First cultivated by Frankfort horticulturalist John Bibb in the mid-1800s, this crisp, buttery variety of lettuce thrived in the limestone-rich soil of Kentucky. Paired with beef tenderloin, a Derby favorite, it makes a tasty salad that works as a meal by itself. In this recipe, I like to use Evan Williams 1783, a top notch bourbon for a bottom shelf price with a deep brown color and herbal flavors that stand up to the bacon and onion in the tart dressing.

2 large heads Bibb lettuce
8 strips bacon
2 small filet mignons
(about 12 ounces total)
1 small yellow onion,
finely chopped
2 tablespoons apple cider vinegar
2 tablespoons spicy brown
mustard
2 tablespoons honey
3 tablespoons bourbon
Salt and cracked black pepper
Tomato wedges for garnish

Wash the lettuce under a stream of cold water. Separate the leaves, pat dry and keep cool. In a heavy skillet over medium heat, cook the bacon until just barely crisp and remove from the pan. Drain off excess fat on a paper towel and crumble when cool. Turn up the heat, and in the same pan, cook the filets that have been seasoned with a bit of salt and pepper for 3–4 minutes on both sides. Remove the steaks from the skillet and cover with a bit of aluminum foil. Drain away all but 2 tablespoons of the fat in the pan, and add the chopped onion and cook until translucent. Turn off the heat and whisk together the vinegar, mustard and honey in the skillet. Add the bourbon and turn up the heat to medium, stirring constantly. When the hot dressing starts to bubble, turn off the heat and season to taste with the salt and pepper. Thinly slice the cooked filets and assemble the salad by arranging the leaves of lettuce on a large serving platter and topping with slices of filet. Drizzle with the hot dressing, sprinkle on the crumbled bacon and garnish with salted wedges of tomato.

The Kentucky Bourbon Festival

Smooth bourbon, delicious food, great entertainment, and a healthy dose of Kentucky hospitality – every year in September, the Kentucky Bourbon Festival in historic Bardstown offers five days full of black tie galas, historical tours, and more. Go online at *www.kybourbonfestival.com* for more information.

4 cups julienned turnip greens
2 cups shredded Savoy cabbage
2 tablespoons spicy
  brown mustard
3 tablespoons apple cider vinegar
1 tablespoon fresh lemon juice
3 tablespoons bourbon
¾ teaspoon kosher salt
½ teaspoon ground black pepper
4 tablespoons canola oil
3 tablespoons extra-virgin
  olive oil
6 large radishes, cut into slivers

Turnip Green Slaw

Since there's no cooking in this recipe, the pure flavors of the whiskey will come through and mingle, so it's good to use a nice sipping bourbon. I like to use Elijah Craig 12 Year Old, a full-bodied bourbon with warm notes of sweet oak and flavors of caramel and rye with a thick finish. Another favorite is sophisticated Jefferson's Reserve, a medium-weight drink with a velvety texture and a dry, robust palate that quickly fills the mouth with hints of roasted corn and toffee. For a less expensive bourbon with the same amount of taste, try Old Bardstown.

Combine the turnip greens and cabbage in a large bowl and set in the refrigerator to keep cool. In a separate bowl, whisk together the mustard, vinegar, lemon juice, bourbon, salt and pepper. Continue whisking and drizzle in the canola and olive oils until the mixture thickens. Pour over the turnip greens and cabbage and toss to coat. Correct the seasoning and mound in a large bowl for service. Top with the slivers of fresh radish and enjoy.

Dandelion Greens with Haricots Verts and New Red Potatoes

Bitter flavors are often shunned today – perhaps because we've become so conditioned to overly sweet and salty processed foods – but in earlier days, bitterness enjoyed more prominence in the kitchen. Mixed with other flavors in a salad, bitter greens such as the dandelion often improve the flavor. This perennial, herbaceous plant has long, lance-shaped leaves that are so deeply toothed, that it was named *dent-de-lion* or lion's tooth in Old French. Although they can be sautéed or steamed, dandelion greens are especially wonderful in salads. With a bitter edge, they taste like chicory and endive and have an intense heartiness that does well with bourbon. For a special treat, try Hancock's President's Reserve in this recipe. Its light palate with hints of spicy lemon and honey make it a wonderful bourbon for dressings.

Place the potatoes in a pot of cold, salted water over high heat and bring to a rolling boil. Let cook for 5 minutes and turn off the heat. Let the potatoes sit in the hot water and continue cooking for another 10 minutes. Blanch the green beans by tossing them into the hot water with the potatoes and removing them after 2-3 minutes. Halve the cooked potatoes. Wash and trim the fresh dandelion greens and place in a large bowl. Toss with the cooled green beans and new red potatoes. Prepare the dressing by first whisking together the mustard, garlic, vinegar, honey, bourbon, salt and pepper. Continue whisking and drizzle in the hazelnut oil, in a thin stream, to emulsify the mixture. Pour over the greens, potatoes and beans and toss to coat well. Correct the seasoning and mound in a large platter for service. Garnish with hazelnuts and sprinkle with cracked pepper.

8 very small new red potatoes
1 pound young green beans
1 bunch fresh dandelion greens
   (about 4 cups)
2 tablespoons brown mustard
1 tablespoon chopped garlic
2 tablespoons red wine vinegar
1 tablespoon honey
3 tablespoons bourbon
½ teaspoon kosher salt
½ teaspoon cracked black pepper
¼ cup hazelnut oil
Toasted hazelnuts for garnish

Baby Spinach with English Peas, Red Pepper and Roasted Garlic

Kentucky Gentleman Bourbon Whiskey adds a nice touch to this salad. It is produced at Barton's Distillery in Bardstown, Kentucky and it has the smooth character and mellow flavor of true bourbon. Consistently ranked among the top bourbon whiskeys in the United States, Kentucky Gentleman enjoys special popularity in the South, particularly in Florida, Alabama and Virginia.

3 heads garlic
½ cup bourbon
Olive oil
Kosher salt and freshly ground black pepper
6 cups fresh baby spinach
2 cups English peas, blanched
1 large red pepper, cut in thin strips
1 tablespoon brown mustard
1 tablespoon honey
1½ tablespoons fresh lime juice
1½ tablespoons bourbon
2 tablespoons balsamic vinegar
3 tablespoons extra-virgin olive oil

Preheat the oven to 375 degrees. Using a very sharp knife, remove the top quarter of each head of garlic to expose the individual cloves. Place the heads of garlic in a small, shallow baking dish. Add the ½ cup bourbon and use a match to carefully flambé the whiskey. (Depending on the proof, the bourbon may not ignite; if not, forgo this step.) Once the alcohol has burnt off and the flame is gone, drizzle each head with a bit of olive oil and sprinkle with the salt and pepper. Cover and place in the oven. After 15 minutes, reduce the heat to 300 degrees and bake for another 30 minutes. Remove from the oven and let the garlic cool, covered, in the pan. Combine the spinach, peas, and red pepper in a large bowl and set aside. When the garlic has cooled, use the point of a sharp knife to individually extract each clove, or else you can squeeze them out with your hands, applying pressure from the bottom and working up to the cut side. Place 6 large roasted cloves in a bowl and mash with the mustard and honey. Whisk in the lime juice, bourbon and vinegar and slowly add the olive oil in a thin stream, continuing to whisk. Season with salt and pepper. Pour the dressing over the greens, tossing to coat. Add the remaining roasted cloves of garlic to the salad, correct the seasoning and enjoy.

Bardstown, Kentucky: Bourbon Capitol of the World

The second-oldest city in the state, Bardstown is quintessential Kentucky. For more than 225 years, the seat of Nelson County has embraced a sense of southern hospitality that has made it famous the world over. With its quaint shops, laid-back manner and friendly residents, it is consistently ranked one of the Best Small Towns in America. Home to the first Catholic diocese in the West, it's been said to have lots of spirit as well. One particular spirit, however, has led to its fame as the Bourbon Capital of the World. With nearby distilleries and an idyllic location at the heart of the Kentucky Bourbon Trail, it's easy to see why. It's also home to the Kentucky Bourbon Festival and the Oscar Getz Museum of Whiskey History.

For more information, contact the
Bardstown-Nelson County Tourist & Convention Commission
at (800) 638-4877.

Photos by James Asher

The Oscar Getz Museum of Whiskey History

In downtown Bardstown, the Oscar Getz Museum of Whiskey History has on display a collection of rare artifacts and documents chronicling the American whiskey industry from pre-Colonial days to post-Prohibition years. In addition to authentic moonshine stills, antique bottles and jugs, the museum includes exhibits on novelty whiskey containers, medicinal bourbon bottles, unique advertising art, and more. The museum shares space with the Bardstown Historical Museum on the main floor of Spalding Hall, part of St. Joseph College and Seminary. Built in the 1820s, the large brick building served as a hospital for both sides in the Civil War and has also been an orphanage and school.

Oscar Getz Museum of Whiskey History
114 North Fifth Street
Bardstown, Kentucky 40004
(502) 348-2999

Photo by Lou Vittitow

Grilled Hearts of Romaine with Bleu Cheese and Black-Eyed Peas

Maker's Mark is known by connoisseurs around the world as a luxuriant, mellow bourbon, its pleasant, clean flavor achieved with the substitution of mild winter wheat for the more common rye used to flavor bourbon. It makes the tangy flavors of the bleu cheese pop in this recipe for grilled salad with black-eyed peas.

3-4 small heads Romaine lettuce
Olive oil
Salt and cracked black pepper
2 tablespoons finely chopped shallot
6 tablespoons red wine vinegar
6 tablespoons bourbon
2 tablespoons honey
6 tablespoons walnut oil
2 cups black-eyed peas, cooked
12 ounces bleu cheese, crumbled

Wash the lettuce and cut each head in half down the middle. Brush generously with the olive oil, sprinkle with the salt and pepper and cook for 2 minutes per side on a medium grill. While the lettuce halves grill, whisk together the shallot, vinegar, bourbon, honey, walnut oil and salt and pepper to taste. Remove the lettuce from the grill and prepare individual salads by topping each lettuce half with black-eyed peas, bleu cheese crumbles and a healthy drizzle of dressing.

Mâche with Sliced Potatoes and Sweet Corn Vinaigrette

Rapunzel, field salad, lamb's lettuce, corn salad, mâche – whatever you call it, this tender salad green with its mild lettuce flavor is little-known in many parts of the country. Cold hardy and able to thrive under extreme weather conditions, it is ideal for harvesting during late fall and early spring when fresh produce is scarce in the garden. In parts of Europe it is often tossed with potato slices and served as a salad along with the main meal. This recipe features bourbon's star ingredient – corn – in its freshest form as a compliment to the corn whiskey in the dressing. Use Early Times, Ancient Age or McAffee's to add a pleasant kick to the vinaigrette. My favorite is Ancient Age, a bottled-in-bond bourbon from Buffalo Trace.

2½ cups fresh sweet corn kernels
1 large clove garlic, smashed
2 tablespoons apple cider vinegar
4 tablespoons bourbon
½ teaspoon kosher salt
¼ cup extra-virgin olive oil
4 large red potatoes, cooked, peeled and sliced
4 cups fresh mâche

In a blender purée ½ cup of the sweet corn with the garlic, vinegar, bourbon, and salt. While blending, slowly drizzle in olive oil until the mixture resembles creamed corn. Toss with the remaining sweet corn, potatoes, and mâche, correct the seasoning and enjoy.

Watercress and Cucumber Spears with Woodford Reserve Citrus Vinaigrette

One of the fastest-growing brands in the country, Woodford Reserve is a premium, small-batch bourbon that has found a home at most decent bars around the world. The brilliant nose warms the palate for subtle intimations of honey, spice and violet – all flavors that do well with the delicate taste of fresh cucumber. The bitter, slightly peppery addition of fresh watercress rounds out this salad that is pulled together with a bracing citrus vinaigrette.

3 large English cucumbers
2 bunches fresh watercress
1 tablespoon brown mustard
1 tablespoon minced shallot
1 tablespoon apple syrup (substitute honey)
Juice of one orange, about 3 tablespoons
Juice of one lemon, about 3 tablespoons
3 tablespoons bourbon
3 tablespoons extra-virgin olive oil
Kosher salt and cracked black pepper

Peel the cucumbers and cut each one into three segments. Cut each segment into 6 spears. Wash the watercress and set aside with the cucumbers to keep cool. To prepare the dressing, use a whisk or a blender to mix together the mustard, shallot, and apple syrup. Add the orange juice, lemon juice, and bourbon. Continue mixing and slowly drizzle in the olive oil to emulsify the vinaigrette. Add the salt and pepper to taste and toss together with the cucumbers and watercress. Season again with salt and pepper and enjoy.

The Kentucky Bourbon Trail: Woodford Reserve Distillery

Nestled amid the picturesque horse farms of the Bluegrass countryside, the Woodford Reserve Distillery has a rich heritage that can be rivaled by few other distilling locations in this country. The site traces the origins of its whiskey production back to 1812, and bourbon-distilling pioneers like Elijah Pepper, Oscar Pepper, and James Crow perfected their craft here. It counts as the smallest and oldest operating distillery in Kentucky

today, the only place where you can find two of the state's most famous exports – bourbon and thorough-bred horses – maturing side-by-side. This National Landmark distillery on the banks of Glenn's Creek is the only in the state to use copper pot stills and matures its bourbon in a unique limestone warehouse.

For information about tours, contact:
Woodford Reserve Distillery
7855 McCracken Pike
Versailles, Kentucky 40383
(859) 879-1812

Photo by James Asher

Cold Brown Salad with Bourbon Buttermilk Dressing

Another take on the famous open-faced sandwich from Louisville's celebrated Brown Hotel, this salad incorporates all the main ingredients of the original, but adds the crisp crunch of iceberg lettuce and the tangy zing of bourbon and buttermilk in the dressing. For that extra punch, try Rebel Yell, a no-nonsense whiskey from Louisville. With every bottle sold, a contribution is made to the Civil War Preservation Trust.

Wash the lettuce and cut into 6-8 wedges. Prepare the dressing by whisking together the buttermilk, mayonnaise, vinegar, bourbon, salt and pepper. Assemble individual salads by laying several slices of tomato over each wedge of lettuce and drizzling with buttermilk dressing. Top with chopped turkey and bacon. Garnish with slivers of Asiago cheese and toast points.

1 head iceberg lettuce
1 cup buttermilk
1 cup mayonnaise
3 tablespoons apple cider vinegar
3 tablespoons bourbon
½ teaspoon kosher salt
¼ teaspoon ground white pepper
2 large tomatoes, sliced
1 small turkey breast, cooked
  and chopped (about 2 cups)
6-8 slices cooked bacon, broken in half
Asiago cheese
Toast points

Bibb Lettuce with Roasted Root Vegetables

Produced at Barton's Distillery in Bardstown, Very Old Barton has a syrupy nose with a sweet, big-bodied palate and random bits of allspice and ginger root. These flavors explode in the tangy, earthy dressing that highlights the robust taste of oven-roasted tubers in this salad. Great any time of year, I especially enjoy it in late summer or early fall.

2 medium red potatoes
2 medium carrots
1 large turnip
1 medium rutabaga
3 tablespoons olive oil
3 tablespoons canola oil
½ teaspoon kosher salt
½ teaspoon cracked black pepper
2 large heads Bibb lettuce
Bourbon Molasses Vinaigrette

Preheat the oven to 450 degrees. Wash and peel the potatoes, carrots, turnip and rutabaga and cut the vegetables in 1-inch pieces. Combine the vegetables in a bowl and toss with the oils, salt and pepper. Once coated, turn the vegetables out onto a baking sheet and roast in the oven for 15 minutes or until the vegetables are golden brown. Remove from the oven and let cool slightly. To assemble the salad, wash and dry the lettuce and arrange on a large serving platter. Add the roasted vegetables and drizzle with the dressing.

Bourbon Molasses Vinaigrette

4 large cloves garlic
2 tablespoons spicy brown mustard
6 tablespoons molasses
3 tablespoons bourbon
3 tablespoons apple cider vinegar
1 teaspoon kosher salt
¼ teaspoon ground white pepper
Juice of one lemon
½ cup extra-virgin olive oil

In a blender, purée the garlic, mustard, molasses, bourbon, vinegar, salt, pepper and lemon juice until smooth. Drizzle in the olive oil while still blending to emulsify the dressing. Correct the seasonings and serve.

Green River Cabbage

The Green River area in western Kentucky is known for its peppery fried fish, and the perfect match to fried fish is cole slaw. This creamy cabbage salad gets an extra kick from a generous dose of cracked black pepper and the bite of W.L. Weller "Antique" 7 Year Old Bourbon, a wheated whiskey known for its big body and spicy, sharp tones.

4 pounds green cabbage, finely shredded
2 large carrots, finely shredded
1 tablespoon kosher salt
¾ cup best-quality mayonnaise
¾ cup sour cream
3 tablespoons bourbon
2 tablespoons honey
2 tablespoons white vinegar
2 tablespoons prepared horseradish
1 teaspoon ground black pepper
½ teaspoon ground white pepper
1 cup frozen corn kernels, thawed

In a large bowl, combine the shredded cabbage, carrots and salt and mix well. Set, uncovered, in the refrigerator for 2 hours so the salt can leach some of the moisture from the vegetables. This will help produce a creamier slaw. Whisk together the mayonnaise, sour cream, bourbon, honey, vinegar, horseradish, and peppers in a medium bowl, and set in the refrigerator to chill for the remainder of the 2 hours. Remove the cabbage mixture from the refrigerator and use your hands to squeeze out as much moisture as you can. Transfer by handfuls to a clean towel and pat dry. Combine with the corn in a large mixing bowl and add the mayonnaise mixture; combine and taste for seasoning. Add more salt, pepper, sour cream or honey as needed.

Main Courses

Free Range Chicken with
  Bourbon and Mission Figs
Bluegrass Schnitzel
Turnip Green Fried Chicken
Trout Gratin
Stuffed Mustard Greens
Green Tomato Pork with
  Yellow Rice
Bourbon Steak Frites
Bourbon Battered Fish with
  Pumpkin Seeds
Chicken Rolls with
  Tomatoes, Bourbon and Cream
Bourbonnaised Filet Mignon

Unless otherwise stated, all recipes are
designed for 6-8 people.

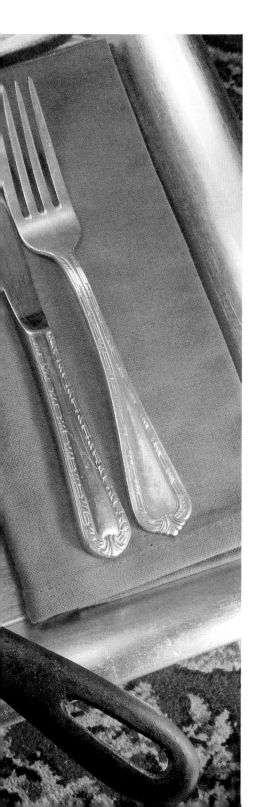

Free Range Chicken with Bourbon and Mission Figs

Although they grow abundantly in many parts of the country, figs first arrived with Spanish missionaries in California. Laden with traces of vanilla, caramel and honey, bourbons tend to have a natural sweetness that marries well with figs. Simmered with a bit of brown sugar, garlic and bourbon such as Knob Creek or Kentucky Tavern, mission figs form the base for a flavorful sauce for slow-cooked chicken. Serve with a simple green salad and Bluegrass Pilaf (page 103) for a satisfying dinner or lunch.

1 large free-range chicken, cut into pieces
  (about 4 pounds)
Salt and freshly ground black pepper
2 tablespoons olive oil
1 large shallot, minced
5 cups fresh mission figs, quartered
2 cups bourbon
⅓ cup apple cider vinegar
½ cup firmly packed dark brown sugar
3 tablespoons fresh lemon juice

Pat the chicken pieces dry and season with the salt and pepper. Heat the olive oil in a Dutch oven over medium-high heat and brown the chicken. Once all the chicken has been browned, add the shallots to the pan, along with the figs, bourbon, vinegar, and sugar. Simmer, covered, over very low heat for 45 minutes. Stir in the lemon juice and season with salt and pepper to taste.

Bourbon or Tennessee Whiskey?

An important American spirit is Tennessee whiskey, Jack Daniels and George Dickel being the leading examples. As far as the distillation process is concerned, it is identical to bourbon whiskey in almost every respect. Tennessee whiskey, however, undergoes an extra filtration process through sugar maple charcoal, which imbues it with a unique flavor and aroma. In 1941, the government of the United States officially recognized Tennessee whiskey as a separate style.

Bluegrass Schnitzel

Wiener Schnitzel. For most speakers of English, it's a somewhat exotic-sounding word with nonsensical overtones, but the dish itself is a rather ordinary concoction. Versions of these breaded meat scallops can be found in many countries around the globe, and chicken-fried steak or breaded pork cutlets would count as distant American cousins of what many consider the quintessential Germanic staple. Translated as "Viennese Cutlet" in English, *Wiener Schnitzel* originated around the 16th century when it most likely arrived in Vienna from nearby Italy. Whatever the background, the preparation is relatively straightforward, as you will see in this Kentucky-fied update of the Austrian original. Try Bulleit Bourbon with this recipe.

1½ pounds pork scallops, pounded thin
¼ cup bourbon
2 large eggs, lightly beaten
1 cup canola oil
½ cup all-purpose flour
1–1½ cups fresh bread crumbs
2 tablespoons spicy brown mustard
Salt and ground white pepper
Thinly sliced country ham or prosciutto
1 lemon, cut in wedges

Place the pork cutlets in a shallow baking dish or a plastic resealable bag with the bourbon and let marinate in the refrigerator for 2 hours. Once the pork has marinated, remove the cutlets and pat them dry, combining the leftover marinade with the two beaten eggs. Set a cast-iron skillet with the canola oil over a medium-high heat, and place the flour, egg mixture, and bread crumbs in 3 individual separate shallow dishes, in that order. Brush each cutlet with a bit of the mustard and season with the salt and pepper. Top with a slice of country ham. To prepare the cutlets, dredge each in flour, shake off the excess and dredge through the egg mixture before coating thoroughly with the fresh bread crumbs. (To ensure an even crust, make sure to firmly press the crumbs onto the pork to make sure they adhere.)

Once the oil has heated enough so that that the end of wooden spoon starts to sizzle when inserted and placed against the bottom of the pan, add 2 or 3 schnitzels to the pan, frying on both sides till golden brown, about 2–3 minutes. Transfer each cutlet to a plate lined with paper towels and place in a 250-degree oven to keep warm. Repeat until all the cutlets have been used, garnish with lemon wedges and dig in. For an Austrian-inspired dinner or lunch, serve the schnitzel alongside a green salad and French fries or with steamed white rice studded with peas. Or, for a great sandwich, slip a schnitzel between the halves of a sliced Kaiser roll and enjoy.

Turnip Green Fried Chicken

A common fall and winter side dish in southeastern cooking in the United States, turnip greens often end up next to a big plate of fried chicken at mealtime. This preparation combines two favorites in a dish that ensures that you'll get a helping of green leafy vegetables. Woodford Reserve makes a nice match to the tangy bitterness of the greens in this recipe.

16 large turnip greens
½ cup bourbon
¾ cup buttermilk
3 tablespoons hot sauce
16 chicken pieces
3 cups all-purpose flour
1 teaspoon kosher salt
½ teaspoon ground turmeric
½ teaspoon ground black pepper
¼ teaspoon dried oregano
¼ teaspoon kosher salt
¼ teaspoon ground white pepper
Canola oil for frying

Lay the turnip greens in a shallow dish or pan and heat the bourbon in a microwave. Pour the hot bourbon over the turnip greens to wilt. Once the bourbon has cooled, pour off and combine with the buttermilk and hot sauce in a large bowl. Add the chicken pieces. Stir to coat well and let marinate in the refrigerator for at least 2 hours. Mix together the flour, 1 teaspoon of salt, turmeric, black pepper and oregano in a large bowl and set aside.

Remove the chicken from the refrigerator and heat the canola oil in a large cast-iron skillet over medium heat. To coat the chicken, it will be best to form a mini assembly line with the chicken, removed from the marinade, in a bowl to the left. Moving to the right, place the dish of seasoned flour, the plate with the turnip greens and then the buttermilk-bourbon mixture.

At the far right, place a large plate to collect the breaded chicken pieces. One at a time, take a piece, shake off the excess moisture and season with a pinch of salt and pepper. Lightly dredge it in flour and wrap it tightly in one of the turnip greens. Dip into the marinade to coat and return to the flour mixture to coat well. Shake off the excess and transfer to a plate while you repeat the process until all pieces have been coated. Fry the pieces in 2 batches until both sides are deep golden brown and remove to a wire rack to drain any excess grease. Enjoy warm or cold.

Trout Gratin

You might not think it, but bourbon and fish can make a great match. Many bourbons have flavors and aromas reminiscent of citrus fruits such as grapefruit and lemon, so the benefits of the pairing is evident. Bourbon can also have a deliciously creamy texture, so its use here with a bit of cream and fresh trout results in a comforting dish that is perfect for brunch or dinner. I like to use Rock Hill Farms, an amber-hued whiskey with sunny aromas of fruit and honey.

6-8 trout filets (about 6 ounces each)
¼ teaspoon kosher salt
¼ teaspoon ground white pepper
2 tablespoons unsalted butter
1 cup heavy cream
¼ cup bourbon
3 tablespoons all-purpose flour
¼ cup grated Parmesan cheese
½ teaspoon kosher salt
½ teaspoon ground white pepper
¼ teaspoon fresh marjoram, finely chopped
1 cup fresh bread crumbs
4 tablespoons unsalted butter

Pat the fish filets dry using a paper towel and season each with the ¼ teaspoon of salt and pepper. Lay in a single layer in a large casserole or baking dish that has been brushed with the butter. Whisk the cream and bourbon together with the flour and mix in the grated cheese, salt, pepper and marjoram. Pour over the fish and sprinkle with the bread crumbs. Dot the surface with teaspoon-size pieces of the butter and bake on the upper rack in a 350-degree oven. Once the surface has turned browned and starts to bubble, about 30 minutes, remove from the oven and let sit for 15 minutes before serving.

Stuffed Mustard Greens

If you don't like mustard greens, try this uncomplicated recipe with turnip greens or Swiss chard instead. A great party food, these flavorful bundles work as an appetizer and main course. Try a good bourbon like Booker's or Wild Turkey Rare Breed, and then enjoy a tumbler of it with the stuffed mustard greens.

1 pound lean ground beef
½ pound country sausage
2 large eggs
2 cups cooked white rice
1 cup grated Parmesan cheese
½ cup grated yellow squash
½ cup grated zucchini
¼ cup chopped green onion
¼ cup chopped fresh parsley
2 tablespoons Worcestershire sauce
2 tablespoons chili sauce
1 teaspoon kosher salt
½ teaspoon ground black pepper
24-30 large mustard greens
1 cup bourbon

Preheat the oven to 375 degrees. In a large bowl, combine the ground beef, sausage, eggs, rice, cheese, squash, zucchini, green onion, parsley, Worcestershire sauce, chili sauce, salt and pepper and mix well. Clean and trim the frilly ends from the mustard greens and heat the bourbon in a small saucepan over medium heat until tiny bubbles start to form around the edge of the pan.

Place the greens in a large shallow dish and wilt by pouring the hot bourbon over them. Remove from the bourbon and let cool. Once the leaves are cool enough to handle, place about 2 tablespoons of the meat filling in the center of each green, fold in the sides and roll up to form a small cylindrical shape. Lay the stuffed greens in a single layer in a large baking dish with the bourbon used to wilt the greens and cook, covered, for about 40 minutes in a 350-degree oven. For a hearty and satisfying dinner, serve stuffed mustard greens with steamed rice and slices of yellow squash. Make a tasty sauce made by puréeing 4 cups chopped tomatoes with the leftover bourbon, trimmed edges from the greens and ½ cup sour cream. This sauce will need to be seasoned and is especially good when cooked and reduced by a third.

Green Tomato Pork with Yellow Rice

Mention green tomatoes, and most people conjure up summertime images of the savory fruit sliced, breaded and fried to simple, crispy perfection. However, many parts of the country use the green tomato in a wide variety of dishes and condiments. Pickled green tomatoes in the northern regions, green tomato relish in the West, green tomato pie in the Midwest and green tomato chow chow in the southern countryside attest to the versatile nature of this rural favorite. In the Mexican-inspired cuisine of the Southwest, tomatillos, a cousin of the green tomato, figure prominently in pork dishes seasoned with spicy local chiles and sweet onion. The tart and tangy notes of fresh green tomatoes pair with the charred overtones of J. W. Dant bourbon to enhance pork in this recipe, which is sure to become a favorite.

3 tablespoons olive oil
4 pounds pork tenderloin, cut in 1 inch cubes
2 tablespoons olive oil
4 large green tomatoes, diced (about 6 cups)
1 large Vidalia onion, diced (about 1½ cups)
4 large cloves garlic, peeled and coarsely chopped
½ cup chopped parsley
½ cup chopped watercress
½ cup pickled banana pepper slices
5 cups chicken stock
¼ cup apple cider vinegar
1 tablespoon kosher salt
1 teaspoon ground white pepper
2 cups bourbon
1 large white onion, halved and sliced
2 large potatoes, peeled and diced

Heat the 3 tablespoons of olive oil in a large, heavy skillet over a high heat and add the pork once the oil starts to smoke. As the meat sears in the pan, heat the 2 tablespoons of olive oil in a large Dutch oven over medium-high heat. While the oil heats, purée the tomatoes, onion, garlic, parsley, watercress, pepper, stock, vinegar, salt and pepper in a blender until smooth. Once the olive oil has started to smoke, add the puréed mixture and cook for 10 minutes. Reduce the heat and simmer for another 5 minutes. After the meat has browned, add the bourbon to the pan and stir to deglaze. Transfer the pork to the pot with the simmering green tomato sauce and add the sliced onion and diced potato. Cook, covered, over very low heat for 2 hours or until the pork cubes have become tender. Correct the seasoning and serve with a steaming helping of savory Yellow Rice.

Yellow Rice

2 tablespoons extra-virgin olive oil
2 tablespoons unsalted butter
4 cups long grain white rice
1½ teaspoons turmeric
4 cups chicken stock
1 cup bourbon
½ teaspoon saffron threads
1½ teaspoons kosher salt
½ teaspoon ground
  white pepper

Heat the olive oil and butter in a large pot over medium heat until the butter has completely melted. Add the rice and stir to coat with the olive oil and butter. Add the turmeric and cook for 5 minutes, stirring often to avoid individual grains of rice from turning brown. Heat the chicken stock and bourbon in a saucepan with the saffron until the broth begins to bubble at the edges of the pan. Pour the hot broth into the pan with the rice and stir well. Add the salt and pepper and cook for 5 minutes as the mixture continues to boil, stirring frequently to avoid sticking on the bottom. Cover the pot, turn off the heat and let sit for 45 minutes. Do not remove the cover, as this will release the steam needed to cook the rice thoroughly. When the

time is up, remove the cover and use a fork to fluff the rice. Correct the seasoning. For an attractive presentation, ladle the pork alongside a serving of yellow rice that has been packed into a small, oiled ramekin and then turned upside down and unmolded.

Bourbon Steak Frites

Bourbon and beef make a wonderful match in the kitchen, no doubt because whiskey works as a natural tenderizer and flavor enhancer. It seems that every country around the world has its classic meat-and-potatoes combination to satisfy hungry appetites, and in the French-speaking world, steak frites would fit the bill. This winning combination of juicy, pan-seared beefsteak with crispy sticks of French-fried potatoes is as likely to be found on the menus of trendy Paris bistros as it is on the farmhouse dinner tables in the Belgian countryside. Paired with Blanton's bourbon and its spicy aromas of dried citrus and cloves accented with burnt sugar, grass-fed beef takes on exceptional flavor in this bistro classic. Booker's and Ezra B. also work well here, but as with most recipes, any bourbon will do.

6-8 small flatiron or strip steaks
1 cup bourbon
4 cups canola oil
2 tablespoons unsalted butter
1 tablespoon kosher salt
1 tablespoon fresh cracked black pepper
6 large russet potatoes, peeled
1½ teaspoons salt
1 tablespoon spicy brown mustard
Juice of one lemon

Place the steaks in a shallow dish and cover with the bourbon. Marinate in the refrigerator for at least an hour. Place a large cast-iron skillet over medium-high heat and add the butter. Heat the oil over medium heat in a large pot or deep fryer. Remove the steaks from the marinade and pat dry. Season each side with the salt and pepper and transfer to the pan once the butter has started to sizzle. Turn the heat up to high and sear the steaks for 3–4 minutes on each side. While the steaks cook, cut each potato lengthwise into 5-6 uniform slices and then cut each of the slices into 5-6 uniform strips. The object is to produce the longest fries possible. Once the oil is hot enough that a piece of potato dropped in starts to sizzle, add the cut fries and stir gently with a wooden spoon. After 2 or 3 minutes, just as the potatoes start to get slightly crisp, remove with a slotted spoon and drain on a lined baking sheet.

Immediately prior to serving the steaks, turn the heat up to high and fry the potatoes again, for 1–2 minutes or until they are golden brown and crispy. Remove from the oil and drain on a lined baking sheet. Sprinkle immediately with salt and serve with the warm steaks. To serve the steaks, remove them from the skillet and keep warm on a plate covered with aluminum foil. Turn the heat up to high and add the leftover marinade, stirring to deglaze the pan. Once the bourbon has reduced by half, whisk in the mustard and lemon juice and top each steak with a spoonful of the pan sauce. Garnish with sliced tomatoes and a spring of fresh dill and enjoy.

Bourbon Battered Fish with Pumpkin Seeds

Pumpkin seeds and bourbon add an unusual twist to this batter-fried fish. Serve with a side of crispy French fries for a fish-and-chip style dinner or enjoy with cole slaw and hushpuppies for a southern supper. Affordable bourbons like Ancient Age, W.L. Weller or Evan Williams work nicely in the batter.

6-8 fish filets (cod, pollock and haddock, for example)
½ cup buttermilk with several dashes hot sauce
Canola oil
½ cup sifted all-purpose flour, seasoned with
  ground white pepper
1½ cups sifted all-purpose flour
⅛ teaspoon baking powder
1 cup soda water
¼ cup bourbon
Kosher salt
1 cup toasted, shelled pumpkin seeds

Lay the fish filets in a shallow dish with the buttermilk and marinate for an hour. In a heavy-duty pot or deep skillet, heat 3 or 4 inches of oil over medium-high heat. While the oil heats, remove the fish from the marinade, dredge in the seasoned flour and set aside. In a medium-size bowl, whisk together the 1½ cups flour, baking powder, water, bourbon and a large pinch of salt. Once the oil has heated enough so that a wooden spoon handle starts to sizzle when inserted into the oil, dip each filet in the batter and remove, shaking off any excess batter. Generously sprinkle each side with the pumpkin seeds and carefully lay each filet in the hot oil. Fry until golden brown on both sides. Remove each fish filet with a slotted spoon and let drain on a plate lined with paper towels or brown paper. Sprinkle immediately with additional kosher salt and enjoy warm with wedges of fresh lemon.

Colonel Albert Blanton

Named in honor of Colonel Albert Bacon Blanton, Blanton's pays tribute to a man who spent a lifetime preserving the tradition of handcrafted bourbon. For more than half a century, Blanton devoted himself not to just the production of fine whiskey, but also the preservation of the heritage of what would become today's Buffalo Trace Distillery.

Raised on a nearby farm, Blanton started work at the distillery in 1897 as an office boy, and by 1921 he had become president of the plant. He also led the company through some of its most trying times and proved instrumental in the exemption that allowed them to continue making whiskey during Prohibition. Under Blanton, the distillery survived the lean times of the Great Depression and the rising waters of the disastrous flood of 1937 as well. (Just a day after the floodwaters receded, Blanton had restored the distillery to normal operations.) It was also the Colonel who kept the distillery going during World War II when it was required to produce straight alcohol for military purposes.

Regarded as a bourbon aristocrat in the mold of the great whiskey barons of the 1800s, Blanton had helped create some of the best bourbons in the world by the time he died in 1959. He always took as much pride in the presentation of the distillery as in the quality of his bourbons, and its rustic setting and natural beauty make the old distillery a popular stop with tourists today.

The Kentucky Bourbon Trail: Buffalo Trace

In Franklin County, just a short distance from the state capitol in Frankfort, millions of buffalo once found passage across the Kentucky River in their move toward the Great Plains. Today, their old trail – or trace – is only a reminder of a time when massive herds roved this country. The spirit of this noble beast, however, lives on at the distillery that now occupies the land where the buffalo used to roam.

For more than two centuries, what is now Buffalo Trace Distillery has kept this spirit alive where a working distillery has been on the grounds since 1787. With 119 acres and 114 buildings, what used to be the George T. Stagg's distillery became Buffalo Trace in June of 1999, when it introduced its flagship bourbon, Buffalo Trace Kentucky Straight Bourbon Whiskey. In 1857, the first modern distillery – the first to incorporate the use of steam power in the production of high quality bourbon – was built on this site. One of Kentucky's original bourbon aristocrats, E.H. Taylor, Jr., purchased the distillery, and he would introduce many advancements in the whiskey industry. In 1886, the distillery saw the introduction of the nation's first climate-controlled warehouse to age whiskey and they soon earned a reputation for producing quality bourbons.

In addition to Buffalo Trace, the distillery produces other award-winning spirits such as Old Charter, Eagle Rare, Blanton's, and W.L Weller. With more than 140 awards including the 2005 "Distiller of the Year" pre-

sented by *Whisky Magazine*, Buffalo Trace claims more international awards than any other North American distillery in the last 20 years.

Buffalo Trace Distillery
1001 Wilkinson Boulevard
Frankfort, Kentucky 40601
(502) 696-5926

Distilling Company, is often credited with developing this concept some 25 years ago. Long-time master distiller Elmer T. Lee had the idea to take especially good barrels and bottle their contents a single barrel at a time, and he managed to persuade the corporate office to go along with his experiment. Under Lee's supervision, the very first single barrel bourbon, Blanton's, hit the market in 1984.

Small Batch

Although most consider single barrel bourbons the cream of the whiskey crop, some find the variance in the levels of quality among barrels a bit too idiosyncratic to warrant individual bottling. Another approach, therefore, to the production of high-quality bourbon is the small batch method. The rationale behind this style is that a person who buys a bottle of bourbon expects each bottle to taste the same. For the proponents of small-batch bourbons, it makes more sense to select the choicest barrels and blend them, instead of bottling them one at a time. The end result is small batch bourbon.

I am a fan of cooking with bourbon but I think it is important to taste the bourbon and its essence. I have tasted many bourbon dishes and 98% of the time I always say after tasting, "needs more bourbon."

Harlen Wheatley, Master Distiller, Buffalo Trace Distillery

Single Barrel

Most distillers produce commercial bourbons as blends of whiskey from different barrels, however distilleries sometimes select a particularly fine-tasting barrel from the center or "heart" of the warehouse and offer a premium bottling from that barrel alone. Known as single barrel bourbon, these whiskeys tend to embody a higher quality of bourbon and derive their inspiration from the phenomenal success of single-malt Scotches. Allowed to age years beyond the average Kentucky whiskey, single barrel bourbon has acquired a reputation as the cream of the crop.

Leestown Distilling, formerly known as Ancient Age

Chicken Rolls with Bourbon, Tomatoes and Cream

The natural sweetness in tomatoes comes to the fore when a healthy dose of bourbon is added to the mix. Reduced with fresh cream, they make a delicious sauce for tender filets of chicken breast meat rolled around bread stuffing and carrots. For this recipe, I like to use a bourbon like Jim Beam Black or Old Pogue.

2 cups fresh bread crumbs
2 tablespoons chopped fresh flat-leaf parsley
2 tablespoons grated Parmesan cheese
¼ teaspoon kosher salt
¼ teaspoon ground white pepper
¼ teaspoon ground marjoram
1 medium egg, beaten
4 large boneless, skinless chicken breasts
1 carrot, cooked and cut into 2-inch sticks
2 tablespoons olive oil
2 tablespoons unsalted butter
28-ounce can whole tomatoes
5 large cloves garlic, minced
½ cup bourbon
2 tablespoons molasses
1 teaspoon kosher salt
½ cup heavy cream

In a small bowl, combine the bread crumbs, parsley, cheese, salt, pepper and marjoram with the beaten egg. Set aside and slice each of the chicken breasts in half lengthwise to form two large cutlets. Use a meat tenderizer to gently pound out the cutlets into flat pieces no more than ¼ inch in thickness. To assemble, mound 2 or 3 tablespoons of the filling onto each cutlet, top with a carrot stick and tightly roll to form small bundles with the seam side down. Heat the olive oil and butter in a heavy skillet over a high heat. Once the butter starts to sizzle, place the rolls, seam side down, in the pan and brown on all sides. Remove the rolls to a platter and keep warm. Break apart the tomatoes and combine with the garlic, bourbon, molasses and salt in a small bowl. Add the mixture to the pan and cook for 10 minutes or until it has thickened slightly. Add the cream, reduce the heat to medium-low and return the chicken rolls to the pan. Simmer, covered, for 15 minutes before correcting the seasoning.

The Old Seelbach Bar

Described as "one of the finest stretches of mahogany in the country" by *The Book of Bourbon* author Gary Regan, The Old Seelbach Bar is a treasure not to be missed when you're in Kentucky. Among its numerous accolades, it had been named "One of the 50 Best Bars in the World." Aside from an enviable collection of whiskeys, guests can enjoy cocktails from the early 1900s and bourbon-inspired cuisine in beautiful turn-of-the-century surroundings.

The Seelbach Hilton
500 South Fourth Street
Louisville, Kentucky 40202
(502) 585-3200

Bourbonnaised Filet Mignon

In Kentucky, it's been said that we'll try splashing bourbon on almost anything, so it's not surprising to find a wealth of whiskey-inspired dishes across the state. However, little by little, bourbon is finding its way into more and more recipes across the nation. Similar to brandy in character, well-aged bourbon can be used in many main course dishes, not to mention in an endless variety of desserts, sides and sauces. Used as a marinade for lean beef tenderloin, bourbon works as a natural tenderizer and flavor enhancer. For a great combination, try Maker's Mark or Wathen's bourbon from the Charles Medley Distillery in Owensboro for this recipe. Blanton's happens to be a favorite here.

Six to eight 4-ounce filet mignons
1 cup bourbon
1 tablespoon freshly squeezed lemon juice
2 tablespoons butter
½ teaspoon kosher salt
1 tablespoon light brown sugar
2 tablespoons brown mustard
¾ cup heavy cream

Lay the filets in a single layer in a shallow dish and pour in the bourbon and lemon juice. Place the dish in the refrigerator and let marinate for at least 4 hours, turning each filet at least once to ensure an even marinade. To cook the filets, melt the butter in a well-seasoned skillet over medium-low heat. Remove the beef from the marinade and pat dry using a paper towel. Season each side with the salt and rub with a bit of the brown sugar. Once the butter has started to sizzle, sear each filet for about 4 minutes on each side. Remove the steaks to a plate and cover with aluminum foil to keep warm. To make the sauce, turn the heat under the skillet up to high and add the leftover bourbon marinade. Once it begins to boil, whisk in the mustard and cream and reduce the sauce by half. Correct the seasoning. Spoon over the filets and enjoy. If desired, serve atop a warm hoecake with white asparagus spears and lima beans. Garnish with halved tomatoes, fresh rosemary and lemon.

Side Dishes

Bourbon Bleu Cheese
  Scalloped Potatoes
Corn and Lima Bean Maque Choux
Squash and Mushroom Gratin
Twice Baked Sweet Potatoes
Baked Cabbage with Country Sausage
  and Chick Peas
Bluegrass Pilaf
Shrimp and White Asparagus
  Casserole
Sour Cream Potatoes with
  Peas and Kale
Bourbon Braised Brussels Sprouts
  with Bacon
Autumn Macaroni and Cheese

Unless otherwise stated, all recipes are designed
for 6-8 people.

Bourbon Bleu Cheese Scalloped Potatoes

I find this recipe works best when you use one of those large, speckle-finished roasting pans with a lid like grandma always used. It will serve a crowd, so don't worry about all that cream. Use a good bourbon such as Knob Creek or Wathen's to work its way through the tang of the bleu cheese and the richness of the cream.

Cooking spray
5 pounds red potatoes,
  peeled and thinly sliced
2 teaspoons kosher salt
1½ teaspoons ground
  white pepper
1 cup all-purpose flour
1 large yellow onion, thinly sliced
½ cup melted butter
8 ounces bleu cheese, crumbled
2 cups heavy cream
1 cup bourbon

Coat the inside of the roasting pan with the cooking spray and spread a layer of potato slices over the bottom of the pan. Sprinkle with a bit of the salt and pepper and roughly 2 tablespoons of flour. Top with several slices of the onion, drizzle a bit of the butter over that and add some of the bleu cheese crumbles. Repeat this process until all those ingredients have been used, reserving a single layer of potatoes for the top. Stir together the cream and bourbon and pour over the potatoes. Cover and bake in a 400-degree oven for at least 45 minutes, or until a knife inserted in the center meets very little resistance. (At this point I like to sneak a taste and gently stir in more salt if necessary.) Uncover and bake for another 10-15 minutes on the top rack for a brown and bubbly top.

Evan Williams Cooking Contest

For more than 20 years, Evan Williams Bourbon has sponsored an annual cooking contest at the Kentucky State Fair in Louisville. Recipes are judged on the name, originality, ease of preparation, appearance, and the use of Evan Williams Bourbon in the taste and aroma of the dish. Each year, contestants submit a wide variety of recipes, and past winners have included Peach Time Summer Soup, Maple-Chipotle Bourbon Glazed Wings, Bayou Beans and Andouille Sausage, and Evan Williams Paella.

For information on how to enter this contest, contact the Kentucky State Fair at (502) 367-5201.

Corn and Lima Bean Maque Choux

The unusual name maque choux probably stems from the French interpretation of the original indigenous name for this vegetable dish of corn, onions and peppers. A traditional dish of southern Louisiana, it's a cousin of succotash and most likely arose as an amalgam of Cajun and Native American cultural influences in colonial times. With the abundance of sweet onion and corn, bourbon seems a natural for this hearty and nutritious sidedish. I like to use Ancient Age 10 Year Old because it brings out the sweetness of the corn and the earthiness of the limas. Add chunks of grilled chicken or jumbo shrimp for a nice main course.

2 tablespoons unsalted butter
1 cup chopped Vidalia onion
½ cup diced red bell pepper
½ cup diced green bell pepper
¼ cup diced celery
4 cups fresh corn kernels
2 cups frozen lima beans, thawed
1 cup bourbon
1 teaspoon kosher salt
½ cup heavy cream

Melt the butter in a large skillet over a medium-high heat and sauté the onions, peppers and celery for 2-3 minutes. Add the corn, limas, bourbon, and salt. Cook, stirring often, until most of the liquid has evaporated. Add the cream and cook for 2 minutes. Remove from the heat, correct the seasoning and serve piping hot with a garnish of chopped parsley.

A Taste for History: The Kentucky Bourbon Trail

History fans and bourbon aficionados can explore the rich tradition and proud past of America's native spirit on the Kentucky Bourbon Trail, a collection of eight distilleries along a picture-perfect drive through the rolling hills of the Bluegrass. Start off in the Frankfort area with Buffalo Trace, Woodford Reserve, Four Roses, and Wild Turkey, and then head over to Bardstown, the Bourbon Capital of the World, for a tour of the Getz Museum, Maker's Mark, Heaven Hill, Jim Beam, and Tom Moore. While experiencing the time-honored process of crafting fine bourbon whiskey, you can also learn the secrets of why Kentucky has the perfect combination of natural conditions that produce the best bourbon in the country.

Photo by James Asher

Squash and Mushroom Gratin

Bourbon brings out the nutty sweetness so characteristic of winter squash in this elegant casserole. For that reason, whiskeys with a nutty palate or finish such as Early Times, Ancient Age or Eagle Rare work especially well in this recipe. My favorite is Four Roses Small Batch, a mellow sipping bourbon with spicy, rich flavors that enhance the goat cheese in this preparation. Serve this dish as a side or pair it with crusty bread and a tossed salad for a nice vegetarian meal.

1 butternut squash (about 1 pound)
1 acorn squash (about 1 pound)
1 cup bourbon
2 large portobello mushrooms
2 tablespoons olive oil
2 tablespoons butter, softened
1½ teaspoons kosher salt
1 teaspoon ground white pepper
½ teaspoon grated nutmeg
2 tablespoons all-purpose flour
4 large cloves garlic, minced
8 ounces fresh goat cheese, crumbled
¾ cup heavy cream
½ cup grated Parmesan cheese

Cut the squash into thin slices after peeling and seeding them. Place in a shallow dish with the bourbon and let marinate. Clean the mushrooms and cut each one into 3–4 thin, diagonal pieces to maximize the surface area. Sauté the pieces in the olive oil over medium-high heat until they shrink a bit and have given up most of their moisture. Add half of the bourbon from the squash to the mushrooms and cook until the liquid has evaporated. Brush a large baking dish with the butter and lay down the butternut squash as the bottom layer. Sprinkle with some of the salt, pepper, nutmeg, garlic, 1 tablespoon of flour and half of the goat cheese. Layer the mushroom pieces over that and repeat the process. Finish with the layer of acorn squash. Mix together the remaining bourbon with the cream and pour over the top. Season with the remaining salt, pepper, and nutmeg and top off with the Parmesan cheese. Cover and bake on the middle rack in a 400-degree oven for 30 minutes, or until the squash has become fork tender. Remove the cover and move the pan to the top rack and bake for another 15 minutes to brown the surface. Let cool for 10 minutes before serving and enjoy.

95

Twice Baked Sweet Potatoes

With the addition of caramelized onions and freshly grated nutmeg, these baked potatoes beg for a good splash of bourbon. One of the more inexpensive bourbons on the market, Mattingly & Moore from Heaven Hill nonetheless has some complex traits that make it a good choice for this recipe. Early Times also works especially well, but for a special treat, use Ridgemont Reserve 1792, a smooth 8-year-old bourbon from Barton Distillery that is named for the year Kentucky became a state.

3-4 large sweet potatoes
2 large Vidalia onions, sliced
2 tablespoons olive oil
½ cup bourbon
1 teaspoon kosher salt
½ teaspoon ground black pepper
½ teaspoon dried thyme
¼ teaspoon ground nutmeg
½ cup sour cream
2 cups shredded Monterey Jack cheese
Fresh chives for garnish

Scrub the potatoes and bake on the middle rack of a 400-degree oven for 30 minutes, or until the flesh has softened noticeably. Remove from the oven and let cool. Sauté the onion with the olive oil in a heavy skillet over medium heat until the onions caramelize, about 30 minutes. Add the bourbon and cook until it has evaporated. Once the potatoes are cool enough to handle, slice each one in half lengthwise and scoop out the contents into a large mixing bowl, making sure to leave enough potato with the skin to form a little boat. Add the sautéed onion, salt, pepper, thyme, nutmeg and sour cream to the potatoes and combine. Stir in half of the cheese and fill each potato skin with equal portions of the mixture. Top with a sprinkle of the cheese and return to the oven for another 15 minutes, or until the cheese has melted and starts to bubble. Garnish with the chives and enjoy.

Bottled in Bond

Only whiskey produced in this country that has been aged and bottled according to strict legal stipulations can be labeled as bottled in bond. These requirements were outlined in the "Bottled in Bond Act," passed by Congress in 1897 and pioneered by Col. Edmund H. Taylor, Jr., a grand-nephew of President Zachary Taylor.

To receive a label as "bottled-in-bond" or "bonded," bourbon must be straight whiskey that is the product of one distillation season and one distiller, and at one distillery. In addition, it must have been stored in a federally bonded warehouse under U.S. government supervision for at least four years and bottled at 100 proof or 50% alcohol by volume. The bottle's label must identify the distillery or distilleries where it was distilled and bottled as well.

The Bottled-in-Bond Act, in effect, made the government in the United States the guarantor of the whiskey's authenticity. As a result, "bottled-in-bond" whiskey came to be regarded as "the good stuff."

The Kentucky Bourbon Trail: Tom Moore Distillery

Very Old Barton, Kentucky Tavern, Kentucky Gentleman, Ten High and 1792 Ridgemont Reserve are produced at the Tom Moore Distillery in Bardstown. Named for the man who founded it in 1879, the distillery still produces the bourbon that bears his name as well. Its star bourbon, 1792 Ridgemont Reserve, is a small-batch bourbon aged for eight years that has a complex taste. Well-balanced and full-bodied, it was named for the year the Commonwealth of Kentucky entered the Union as the 15th state. Like the other bourbons produced at Tom Moore Distillery, water from the same spring used by its founder goes into every barrel.

To arrange a tour, contact:
Tom Moore Distillery
300 Barton Road
Bardstown, Kentucky 40004
(502) 348-3774

Baked Cabbage with Country Sausage and Chick Peas

Old Grand-Dad Whiskey consistantly ranks among the top-selling straight whiskies. Distilled at the Booker Noe Plant in Boston, Kentucky, it is a Jim Beam brand today. Raymond B. Hayden – grandson of distiller Basil Hayden, Sr. – founded the original company and named the brand after his famous grandfather, whose likeness can be seen on each bright orange label. The Hayden family's first commercial distillery was established in 1840, and the bourbon has been in production ever since. Old Grand-Dad comes in three different strengths – 86 proof, 100 proof "Bonded" and 114 "Barrel Proof" – and any of them will work in this hearty dish.

1 pound country sausage
1 large red onion, cut in half and sliced
1 head cabbage (about 3 pounds)
¼ cup red wine vinegar
1 cup bourbon
½ cup apple juice
3 tablespoons dark brown sugar
½ teaspoon red pepper flakes
2 cups cooked chick peas
Salt and ground black pepper

Break the sausage into chunks and brown in a Dutch oven over medium heat. Drain off any excess fat and add the onion. Cut the cabbage in half and remove the core. Cut each half into 4 wedges and add to the onion and sausage. Mix the vinegar with the bourbon, apple juice, and brown sugar and pour over the cabbage. Add the pepper flakes, cover and bake in a 400-degree oven for 45 minutes. Add the chick peas and cook, uncovered, for another 15 minutes, braising the cabbage in the liquid from time to time. Season with salt and pepper and enjoy.

Bluegrass Pilaf

Pilaf is a dish rooted in Turkish and Persian cuisine in which a grain, such as cracked wheat or rice, is browned in oil, and then cooked with broth and seasonings. Depending on the local tastes, it may also contain a variety of meats and vegetables. This version incorporates country ham and Kentucky's native spirit for a new twist on an old standard. Jim Beam works especially well here.

2 tablespoons olive oil
3 tablespoons unsalted butter
3 cups jasmine rice
¼ cup finely chopped red onion
¼ cup finely chopped parsley stems
3 large cloves garlic, minced
½ cup country ham, finely diced
   (may substitute prosciutto)
1 cup bourbon
4½ cups hot chicken broth
1 cup dried red lentils
Kosher salt and ground black pepper

In a large Dutch oven or heavy covered pot, heat the olive oil and butter over a medium heat. Add the rice and fry the mixture for 5 minutes, stirring often. Add the onion, parsley, garlic, and country ham, and sauté until the onions begin to soften. Add the bourbon and turn up the heat to high, careful that the bourbon doesn't ignite. (If it does ignite, simply cover the pot and extinguish the flame. You could also add some chicken broth to the bourbon to dilute it before adding it to the pan.) Once most of the bourbon has cooked off, add the broth and stir while the mixture boils for 2 minutes. Stir in the lentils, cover the pot and place in an oven preheated to 350 degrees. Bake for 20

minutes. Remove from the oven and let sit for at least 10 minutes before taking off the lid. When the time comes, remove the lid and fluff the rice with a fork to separate the grains. The chicken broth and the country ham should have enough salt already, but you should check the pilaf and correct the seasoning with salt and pepper, especially if you decide to use something other than country ham.

Shrimp and White Asparagus Casserole

Fresh asparagus used to be a sign of spring, but nowadays it is available any time of year. The tender shoot of a plant in the lily family, asparagus has a one-of-kind flavor and comes in three colors: green, white, and purple. White asparagus – asparagus that has been covered with soil during the growing process to prevent the development of green pigmentation – is especially sweet when paired with bourbon and shrimp in this easy recipe. I like to use an elegant bourbon like Willett Family Pot Still Reserve in this dish.

2 pounds fresh white asparagus
½ cup bourbon
2 pounds fresh, whole medium-size shrimp
½ cup chopped fresh spinach
1 tablespoon minced garlic
2 large eggs
1 cup heavy cream
½ teaspoon kosher salt
½ teaspoon ground white pepper
¼ teaspoon fresh grated nutmeg
2 cups coarse, fresh bread crumbs
2 cups grated Asiago cheese
2 tablespoons olive oil
2 tablespoons melted butter

Preheat the oven to 375 degrees. Clean and trim the asparagus spears and cut them in ½-inch pieces. Transfer to a saucepan with the bourbon and cook, covered, over medium heat for 5 minutes or until the asparagus has softened slightly. Drain off the liquid and reserve while the asparagus cools. Clean and devein the shrimp. Toss the shrimp and asparagus together with the chopped spinach and garlic. Beat the eggs and whisk into the cooled bourbon poaching liquid. Add the cream, salt, pepper and nutmeg and pour over the shrimp and asparagus mixture. Fold in 1 cup of the bread crumbs and 1 cup of cheese and set aside. Use a pastry brush to grease a large casserole or skillet with the olive oil and coat the bottom and sides of the dish with another ½ cup of the bread crumbs. Pour in the shrimp-and-asparagus mixture and top with the remaining 1 cup of cheese. Toss the remaining bread crumbs with the melted butter and sprinkle over the cheese and bake, uncovered, for 25 minutes or until the top has become brown and bubbly.

Sour Cream Potatoes with Peas and Kale

Kale, or borecole, is one of those vegetables that doesn't get enough attention in today's kitchen. It's actually a form of cabbage where the central leaves do not form a head and falls in the same species as broccoli, cauliflower and brussels sprouts. Extremely nutritious with numerous anti-oxidant and anti-inflammatory properties, kale adds a robust flavor to this dish, while cutting down on the number of carbohydrates. Try it as a side to your next plate of meatloaf or corned beef, and wash it down with a tumbler of good bourbon. I like to use Jim Beam's Distiller's Select.

4-5 large red potatoes
  (about 3 pounds)
½ cup bourbon
2 cups chopped fresh kale
2 cups frozen peas, thawed
2 cups sour cream
2 teaspoons salt
1 teaspoon ground white pepper
¼ teaspoon freshly ground nutmeg

Peel the potatoes and cut into ½-inch cubes. Cook in boiling salted water until the potatoes are fork tender. Strain off the water and add the bourbon and kale to the pot; cover and let steam for several minutes. Add the peas, sour cream, salt, pepper, and nutmeg. Stir to combine and let sit, covered, for several minutes before serving.

Bourbon Braised Brussels Sprouts with Bacon

The green, leafy buds of the brussels sprout resemble miniature heads of cabbage and they have an intense, somewhat bitter flavor. This might be the reason many people profess to dislike this vegetable high in vitamin C. Overcooking releases a sulphur-smelling glucosinolate known as sinigrin, so this could actually be the culprit. Braised with bacon and a bourbon such as Old Bardstown, these sprouts aquire a mellower flavor that can make the staunchest critic a fan.

½ pound hickory-smoked bacon, chopped
2½ pounds fresh brussels sprouts
¼ cup sliced shallots
1 cup bourbon
½ cup apple juice
2½ tablespoons honey
Kosher salt
Freshly ground black pepper

In a heavy skillet, cook the bacon over medium heat until it browns. Clean the sprouts and cut off the tough ends, using a paring knife to cut a little criss-cross on the bottom of each. (This will help the sprouts cook faster.) Drain away most of the bacon fat from the pan and add the sprouts and shallots. Stir often. When the shallots start to caramelize, add the bourbon, which has been mixed together with the apple juice and honey. Turn up the heat. When the liquid starts to boil, turn the heat down and simmer, covered, for 30 minutes, or until the braising liquid has reduced by half and the sprouts have become tender. Add the salt and black pepper to taste and enjoy.

Autumn Macaroni and Cheese

Homemade macaroni and cheese is one of those comfort foods – like meat loaf, mashed potatoes, fried chicken and freshly baked bread – that possesses the power to satisfy serious cravings for both nostalgia and something warm and gratifying. Fortunately, creamy and rich macaroni and cheese made from scratch can be enjoyed any time of year; however, it holds a special allure when the sun has gone down early on a frosty winter's evening or a cool fall night. The warm, inviting flavors of bourbon, molasses and nutmeg round out this satisfying dish with a distinctive twist of fall. Affordable bourbons like Heaven Hill work well here, but since the recipe only calls for a single cup, I like to splurge every now and then and use a top-shelf bottle like Basil Hayden's.

1½ pounds dried extra-large elbow macaroni
  (about 7 cups)
3 tablespoons unsalted butter
3 tablespoons olive oil
½ cup all-purpose flour
1 cup bourbon
4 cups heavy cream
1 pound extra-sharp white Cheddar cheese, shredded
1 pound extra-sharp yellow Cheddar cheese, shredded
½ cup grated Parmesan cheese
2 tablespoons blackstrap molasses
2 tablespoons apple cider vinegar
2 tablespoons minced garlic
2 teaspoons kosher salt
1½ teaspoons ground white pepper
½ teaspoon freshly grated nutmeg

Cook the pasta according to the package directions. As the elbows cook, melt the butter with the olive oil in a large saucepan over a medium heat. Add the flour and cook, stirring often, for 5 minutes or until the roux has turned golden brown. Turn the heat up to medium-high and whisk in the bourbon to remove all lumps. When the mixture starts to bubble, whisk in the cream and reduce the heat to medium-low. Cook for 5 minutes, stirring often, until the mixture has thickened somewhat. Stir in the cheeses until melted, then stir in the molasses, vinegar, garlic, salt, pepper, and nutmeg. By this time, the macaroni should have cooked. Strain and return to the pan, stirring now and then to prevent it from sticking together. Add the cheese sauce and combine. Pour into a large buttered casserole dish and bake in a 425-degree oven for 20 minutes or until the top browns and starts to bubble.

Breads

Unless otherwise stated, all recipes
 are designed to feed 6-8 people.

Bourbon Poppy Seed Rolls

The seeds of the *papaver somniferum* are widely consumed throughout countries in Europe and the Middle East where they flavor cakes, breads, and cookies. In Turkey, they are often ground and used in desserts, and in India, they use the seeds to thicken sauces. They also flavor a variety of noodle, fish, and vegetable dishes in Jewish cooking. Tiny and nutty-tasting, these blue-gray seeds add a savory touch to yeast rolls, especially when combined with a good bourbon like Ezra B., a single-barrel bourbon aged for 12 years.

2 cups warm water
1½ tablespoons active dry yeast
2 tablespoons granulated sugar
6-7 cups all-purpose flour
1 cup bourbon
2 tablespoons vegetable oil
1 tablespoon salt
1 egg white
1 teaspoon bourbon
½ cup poppy seeds

In a large bowl, stir together the water, yeast, sugar and 2 cups of the flour. Let sit until bubbles start to form on the surface. Pour the bourbon into a deep, microwaveable glass or plastic bowl and heat for 4-5 minutes in the microwave or until the bourbon has reduced by half. (You may also do this in a pan on the stove, but you will need to be careful, especially around open flames.) Cool and add the bourbon to 2 cups of the remaining flour and stir to form a crumbly mix. Combine with the yeast mixture and mix well to remove any lumps. Add the oil, salt and enough flour to form a sticky dough. Turn out onto a floured surface and knead until the dough becomes soft and elastic, about 10 minutes. Place the dough in a greased bowl and let rise, covered, in a warm place until doubled in bulk, at least 1 hour. After the dough has risen, punch down and divide into 12-18 equal portions. Whisk together the egg white and 1 teaspoon bourbon. Place the poppy seeds on a plate. Shape each portion of dough into a ball and brush the top of each with a bit of egg white. Carefully press the top of each roll into the poppy seeds to coat. Place the rolls on a parchment-lined baking sheet and let rise for another hour. Bake in a 400-degree oven for 20 minutes, or until golden brown.

Water of Life

Many believe the word "whisky" came about in the 12th century when soldiers of King Henry II struggled to pronounce native Irish words after they invaded Ireland. Especially daunting was the Gaelic word for the local spirit - *uisce beatha*. The name is a Gaelic translation of the Latin phrase "aqua vitae" or "water of life." Over time, the pronunciation changed from "whishkeyba" (an approximation of the pronounciation of the Irish term) to "whisky."

Bourbon Brioche

This rich French bread gets its tender crumb from a relatively high content of butter and egg; the flaky crust comes from an application of egg wash before baking. When baking, you can choose two common forms: brioche à tête, the most recognized form, has loaves or rolls panned in fluted tins with a spherical piece of dough on top; brioche nanterre is baked in a standard loaf pan, with two rows of small pieces of dough fused together during the baking process to form an attractive pattern. I like to use Buffalo Trace in this recipe.

¼ cup very warm water (110°–115°F)
1 cup granulated sugar
1 tablespoon active dry yeast
2½ cups cake flour
3 cups all-purpose flour
1 tablespoon salt
6 large eggs, at room temperature
½ cup bourbon
10 ounces unsalted butter,
  cut into 1-inch cubes, softened
Butter to grease baking pans

Combine the water, sugar and yeast in a small bowl. Let stand for 10 minutes until the yeast is completely dissolved. Set aside. Sift together the flours and salt into the bowl of a stand mixer fitted with the dough hook. Add the eggs, one at a time, and the bourbon, and beat for 1 minute at low speed, scraping down the sides of the bowl with a rubber spatula as needed. Slowly add the dissolved yeast and continue beating at low speed for 5 minutes. Stop the machine, scrape any dough off the hook, and beat for another 5 minutes. Add several of the butter cubes at a time, beating for about 1 minute after each addition. Once all the butter has been added, beat for an additional 10 minutes. Place the dough in a large bowl brushed with extra butter on the inside and cover with plastic wrap. Set aside in a warm place until doubled in size, about 3 hours.

Turn the dough out onto a floured surface and gently fold over several times to work out the air bubbles. Return to the bowl, cover with plastic wrap, and refrigerate overnight. Generously butter 2 large brioche pans or ramekins (8-inch diameter) and turn the dough out onto a floured surface. With floured hands, divide the dough into three portions. Shape 2 of the portions into balls and place in the ramekins. Use a sharp knife to make a 3-inch slit across the surface of each ball. Take the remaining portion of dough and divide in half. Shape each piece into a smaller ball and insert it into the slit on each portion of dough. Let the dough rise, uncovered, in a warm place until doubled in size, about 3 hours. Brush the tops with a bit of bourbon-egg wash and sprinkle with a bit of sugar. Bake the brioche in the center of a 350-degree oven until golden brown on top, 35–40 minutes. Remove the brioche from the oven and immediately turn out onto a wire rack.

Bluegrass Harvest Bread

Two long proofs and lots of yeast are needed to help rise this incredibly dense – and equally flavorful – bread studded with raisins, seeds and nuts. Because it has nice flavors of spice and sweet corn, I like to use Henry McKenna, the only extra-aged, bottled-in-bond, single-barrel bourbon out there. Be adventurous, though, and see what brand works best for you.

2 cups rolled oats
½ cup cornmeal
½ cup chopped raisins
1 cup bourbon
2 cups boiling water
3 tablespoons dry yeast
½ cup honey
½ cup unsulfured blackstrap molasses
1 cup warm water
3-4 cups bread flour
1 cup whole wheat flour
1 cup shelled pumpkin seeds
¾ cup finely chopped walnuts
2½ tablespoons kosher salt
½ teaspoon ground cinnamon
½ teaspoon freshly grated nutmeg

In a large bowl, mix oats, cornmeal, and raisins with the bourbon and set aside while the water boils. Add the boiling water, stir well, and let cool. In a large mixing bowl stir together 1 tablespoon of the yeast with the honey, molasses, warm water and 1 cup of the flour to form a slurry; set aside for 5 minutes to activate the yeast. When the surface of the mixture develops a bit of foam and small bubbles, you will know the yeast has been activated. Add the slurry to the honey-oat-corn mixture and combine. Add whole wheat flour, pumpkin seeds, walnuts, and 2 cups of the bread flour. Mix well, adding the salt, cinnamon, nutmeg, and remaining yeast just as the dough starts to come together. Turn out onto a board or countertop and knead for 10-15 minutes, incorporating as much additional flour as necessary to form a sticky, elastic dough. Wash out the large mixing bowl, grease with a bit of oil, and return the dough to it. Cover with plastic wrap or a damp dishtowel and set in a warm place to rise overnight, or at least 8 hours. Remove from the bowl, knead once or twice, and divide the dough into 2 portions. Form oblong loaves and place each on a baking sheet that has been slightly greased. Sprinkle with a bit of cornmeal and some extra pumpkin seeds and make several diagonal slits across the top with a sharp knife. (You may choose to use loaf pans instead.) Let loaves rise for another 8 hours, or until doubled in size once again. Preheat the oven to 400 degrees and bake on a middle rack for 35 minutes, or until the surfaces are dark brown and crusty.

The Kentucky Bourbon Trail: Heaven Hill

At the elegant white oak and limestone Bourbon Heritage Center for America's largest independent family-owned producer of distilled spirits, visitors are invited to explore the birth of bourbon and the role of whiskey-making pioneers such as Evan Williams and Elijah Craig. Guests experience the process by which award-winning bourbons are produced through interactive exhibits and tours of rickhouses storing one of the world's largest bourbon inventories. Aside from Elijah Craig and Evan Williams, Heaven Hill has produced bourbons such as Henry McKenna and Old Fitzgerald since it was founded in 1934.

For more information, contact:
Bourbon Heritage Center
1311 Gilkey Run Road
Bardstown, Kentucky 40004
(502) 337-1000

Photo from Heaven Hill Distillery

115

Right: Plumb bobs (lower part of picture) are used to insure equal weight distribution when bourbon barrels are removed from warehouses.

Photo from Heaven Hill Distillery

Savory Pumpkin Bread

This delicious yeast-risen bread is a welcome alternative to the rich, sweet quick bread variety. Delicious on its own with butter or olive oil, it also makes fine sandwiches and fabulous toast. For a nice baking bourbon, try Jim Beam or Evan Williams.

2 tablespoons active dry yeast
1 cup warm water
½ cup granulated sugar
½ cup molasses
4 cups unbleached all-purpose flour,
   plus additional flour for kneading
2 cups canned pumpkin purée
1 cup bourbon
1½ tablespoons salt
½ teaspoon ground ginger
2 cups whole wheat graham flour

Mix the yeast, water, sugar, molasses and 1 cup of the all-purpose flour together in a large bowl, stirring to combine and dissolve. In another bowl, stir together the pumpkin purée, bourbon, salt, and ginger; set aside. Once the yeast mixture has started to produce bubbles, add the whole wheat flour and pumpkin mixture and mix well. Add another cup of the all-purpose flour and stir with a large, sturdy spoon until the flour is incorporated and dough starts to leave the sides of the bowl. Turn out onto a floured surface and incorporate as much remaining flour as necessary, kneading until dough is smooth and satiny, about 10 minutes. Clean and lightly oil the bowl and return the dough. Cover with a clean, damp tea towel and set in a warm place to rise. Let rise until doubled, at least 1 hour. To form the loaves, punch down the dough and reserve about 2 tablespoons for later. Divide the remainder into 2 equal portions. Shape each into a round

loaf and place on lightly oiled baking sheets. Using a very sharp knife, work your way around the loaf and every inch or so, make a vertical slit from the bottom to the top to simulate the lines on a pumpkin. Finish it off with a piece of the leftover 2 tablespoons of dough that has been fashioned into a stem and inserted into a small slit on the top of the loaf. Cover each loaf with a tent made of aluminum foil and let rise until doubled. Bake at 400 degrees for about 35 minutes, or until browned on top and the bottom sounds hollow when tapped. Cool on a wire rack.

Wild Turkey Crumpets

The addition of baking powder to a thin yeast dough results in the distinctive flat top and characteristic small holes of this crumpet. An Anglo-Saxon invention, crumpets started off as hard pancakes cooked on a griddle and evolved into the spongy crumpets popularized in the Victorian era. By themselves, they're somewhat bland, but with a dab of butter and strawberry jam, they can't be beat. Wild Turkey bourbon adds a grainy bitterness that makes a perfect backdrop for either a sweet or savory topping.

with both the top and bottom removed.) Place rings on the cooking surface and preheat over a medium heat. Pour 3 tablespoons of the batter into each ring and cook until set, about 7-10 minutes. The surfaces will be full of holes when ready to turn. Remove the crumpets from the rings, turn, and brown the other side for another minute or two. Repeat until all the batter is used. Depending on the thickness of the crumpet, you may want to cut them in half before serving. They are even better when you toast them after splitting.

2 tablespoons honey
½ cup warm water (105°-115°F)
1 tablespoon active dry yeast
2½ cups all-purpose flour
¼ cup granulated sugar
1 teaspoon salt
½ teaspoon baking powder
1 cup milk
½ cup bourbon

In a large bowl, stir the honey into the warm water and whisk in the active dry yeast; let sit until it starts to foam, about 5 minutes. Stir in the remaining ingredients to form a thick batter. Cover and let sit for 30 minutes in a warm place. Grease a griddle or frying pan and the crumpet rings. (If you don't have crumpet rings, use cleaned tuna cans

Bacon Rolls

I get invited to potlucks and holiday parties on the condition that I bring these rolls along. It's amazing what a little bacon does. Although a whole pound is called for, this recipe breaks down to a third or a half strip of bacon per roll, depending on the size you make. So, relax, it's not really that much pork fat in the grand scheme of things. I generally rely on Evan Williams for most of my bread recipes, however, I have been known to indulge every now and then and use a bottle of Baker's, a remarkably smooth and intensely flavorful bourbon that's aged for seven years. The best part is the glass I pour myself while I'm waiting for the rolls to rise.

1 pound bacon, diced
½ cup bourbon
2 cups warm water
1 tablespoon dry yeast
2 tablespoons sugar
5-6 cups all-purpose flour
3 tablespoons vegetable oil
2 teaspoons kosher salt

Preheat the oven to 400 degrees. In a heavy skillet over medium heat, fry the bacon until it starts to brown; do not make it too crisp. Drain off most of the grease and reserve it for later. Add the bourbon to the pan with the bacon and cook until most of the liquid has evaporated. In a large mixing bowl, mix 1 cup of the water with the yeast, sugar, and 1 cup of the flour, and set aside for 5 minutes. Once bubbles have started to appear on the surface, stir in 2 cups of the flour, the remaining water, and the bacon. Add the oil and salt and another cup of the flour and stir. When the dough starts to pull away from the sides of the bowl, turn out onto a floured surface, and knead, incorporating

enough of the remaining flour to form a soft, elastic dough. Knead for 10 minutes more. Wash out the mixing bowl and generously grease the sides of the bowl with a bit of the bacon grease. Return the dough to the bowl and cover with a damp dishtowel. Let rise in a warm place for an hour, or until double in size. Once the dough has risen, turn out onto a lightly floured surface and knead once or twice. Use the leftover bacon fat to grease the sides of 24 regular-size or 36 miniature-size muffin cups. Depending on the size of the pan you use, divide the dough into 24 or 36 equal portions and roll each piece of dough into a ball and place it into the individual molds. Let rise for at least another hour and bake for 15 minutes or until golden brown. Remove from the oven and let sit for 2 minutes in the pans before transferring to a rack to cool.

Oatmeal Bourbon Loaves

This hearty brown bread gets its sweetness from molasses and the mellow caramel flavors of McAffe's Benchmark Bourbon, a not-overly complex bargain whiskey made at Buffalo Trace Distillery in Frankfort. If you can't get your hands on a bottle, try a bourbon that smells good to you. Deep amber, almost bronze in color with a sweet nose and rich tones of butterscotch and caramel, Pure Kentucky XO Bourbon also works well here.

3 cups rolled oats
1 cup bourbon
2 cups boiling water
1 tablespoon dry yeast
½ cup molasses
1 cup warm water
4-6 cups bread flour
1 tablespoon salt

In a large bowl, mix 2 cups of the oats with the bourbon and let sit while the water boils. Add the boiling water, stir well, and set aside to cool. In a second mixing bowl stir together the yeast with the molasses, warm water and 1 cup of the flour to form a slurry; set aside for 5 minutes to activate the yeast. If the surface of the mixture develops a bit of foam and small bubbles, you will know the yeast has been activated. Add the slurry to the cooled oat batter and combine. Add 3 cups of the flour and mix well, adding the salt just as the dough starts to come together. Turn out onto a board or countertop and knead for 10–15 minutes,

incorporating as much additional flour as necessary, to form a satiny, elastic dough. Wash out a mixing bowl, grease with a bit of oil, and return the dough to it. Cover with plastic wrap or a damp dishtowel and let rise in the refrigerator overnight. Remove from the bowl, knead once or twice, and divide the dough into 3 portions. Form oblong loaves and roll each in the leftover oats to coat. Place each on a baking sheet that has been sprinkled with oats. Let the loaves rise for another 3 hours or until double in size once again and preheat the oven to 400 degrees. Bake on a middle rack for 25 minutes, or until the surfaces are deep brown and crusty.

121

Cheese Chive and Garlic Pone

With their dense, grainy texture, these crispy corn sticks make the perfect side to a bowl of steaming chili or plate of collard greens. Good bourbons for this recipe include Rebel Yell, Kentucky Tavern, and Jim Beam. If you want to splurge, try Buffalo Trace or Four Roses Single Barrel.

2 cups finely ground yellow cornmeal
2 tablespoons granulated sugar
½ cup bourbon
3 tablespoons minced garlic
1 cup boiling water
2 tablespoons vegetable oil
1 teaspoon salt
½ teaspoon baking powder
1 cup grated Parmesan cheese
1 small egg, slightly beaten
¼ cup fresh chives
Vegetable oil

Mix cornmeal, sugar and bourbon together in a bowl and add the garlic. Heat water to boiling and stir in the cornmeal mixture. Cook for 5 minutes and let cool. Add the vegetable oil, salt, baking powder, Parmesan cheese, egg, and chives. Mix well. Preheat the oven to 400 degrees. Divide the dough into equal portions. Shape each portion into a stick about 3 inches long and bake on a greased cookie sheet for 30 minutes or until golden brown. Or, to make a large pone, place 2 tablespoons of oil in the bottom of a small cast-iron skillet and heat in the oven. Once the pan is hot, pour in the cornmeal mixture and spread to fill the bottom of the pan. Bake for about 40 minutes or until golden brown.

Hoecakes

Legend has it that hoecakes, a traditional cornmeal-based bread, originated in the American South when cooks used the blades of hoes to cook them over an open fire. They can be eaten with butter and syrup for breakfast, and they are often enjoyed with typical southern dishes such as fried chicken or country ham. For something a little different, use them instead of sliced bread to make sandwiches. They also make a nice cushion under a grilled steak or pork chop. Good bourbons for this recipe include Rebel Yell, Old Fitzgerald and Evan Williams 1783.

1 tablespoon granulated sugar
1 cup self-rising cornmeal
1 cup self-rising flour
1 teaspoon salt
Clarified butter for frying
¼ cup vegetable oil
¼ cup hot water
¼ cup bourbon
½ cup buttermilk
2 eggs, beaten

In a large bowl, mix the sugar, cornmeal, flour and salt together until combined. Heat the butter in a large skillet over a medium heat. Mix together the oil, water, bourbon, buttermilk, and stir into the dry ingredients until incorporated. Add the eggs and mix well. Drop 2 tablespoons of the batter into the hot skillet for each hoecake. Fry each cake until brown and crisp; turn with a spatula, and brown the other side. Remove each hoecake and enjoy warm.

Lemon Muffins

Meyer lemons work best in this recipe because they are extra sweet and play nicely off the sugary characters of bourbon. Native to China – and thought to be a cross between a true lemon and a sweet orange – the Meyer lemon was introduced to this country in 1908, when agricultural explorer Frank Meyer, an employee of the United States Department of Agriculture, brought it back from a trip to Asia. Bourbons that work well here are Elijah Craig Single Barrel, Heaven Hill and Yellowstone.

2 cups all-purpose flour, sifted
1½ cups granulated sugar
2 teaspoons baking soda
1 teaspoon salt
2 large Meyer lemons
¾ cup bourbon
2 large eggs
½ cup buttermilk
½ cup melted unsalted butter

Preheat the oven to 400 degrees. In a large bowl, whisk together the flour, sugar, baking soda and salt. Trim off the stem end from the lemons and cut into 1-inch pieces, carefully removing the seeds. Put the pieces, peel and all, in a food processor with the bourbon and process until finely chopped. In a medium bowl, lightly beat the eggs. Add the buttermilk, butter and lemon-bourbon mixture and stir to combine. Pour the lemon mixture into the flour mixture and mix until moistened. Coat 12-15 regular-size muffin molds with butter and fill each ¾ full. Bake for about 20 minutes, or until muffins are light golden. Cool for 2 minutes in the pan, then run a butter knife around muffins to loosen and transfer to a rack to cool.

Photo by James Asher

Kentucky Bourbon Distillers, Ltd.

Many thought it was a sad day for the bourbon world when the old Willett Distilling Company outside of Bardstown, Kentucky, closed down in the 1980s. The Willetts, Kentucky Bourbon aristocrats with a distilling lineage going back several centuries, had built the distillery in 1935 and it was their time to retire. But on July 1, 1984, Even Kulsveen, a native of Norway and son-in-law to Thompson Willett, purchased the property from the Willetts and formed Kentucky Bourbon Distillers, Ltd. After years of painstaking restoration and reconstruction, the historic site continues to produce world-class whiskeys such as Johnny Drum and Willett Family Pot Still Reserve in the heart of Bourbon Country.

For more information, contact:
Kentucky Bourbon Distillers, Ltd.
1869 Loretto Road, P.O. Box 785
Bardstown, Kentucky 40004
(502) 348-0081

Sweets

Angel Crunch Cake
Blue Monday Ice Cream
Apple Bourbon Upside Down Cake
Repeal Day Pound Cake
Orange Bourbon Crème Brûlée
Johnny Drum
Whiskey Truffles
American Honey Cheesecake
Bourbon Ball Torte
Ginger Bourbon Lace
  with Chantilly Cream and
  Fresh Fruit

Unless otherwise stated, all recipes are
designed for 6-8 people.

Angel Crunch Cake

Bourbon is a natural for any sweet dish. Bakery goods with bourbon are especially good, especially when they've had a day or two to age and let the flavors marry. This simple cake with its crunchy-chewy top makes a great wake-up treat in the morning with a cup of coffee, or it can be served with a cup of tea in the afternoon. For baking cakes, try a bourbon with lots of vanilla such as Wild Turkey Rare Breed or Elijah Craig 12 Year Old.

1½ cups cake flour
¾ cup granulated sugar
½ teaspoon baking soda
½ teaspoon baking powder
¼ teaspoon salt
8 tablespoons unsalted butter, slightly softened
2 large eggs
1 teaspoon vanilla extract
¾ cup bourbon
½ cup buttermilk
Cooking spray
¼ cup granulated sugar
¾ cup light brown sugar
½ teaspoon ground cinnamon
½ teaspoon salt
8 tablespoons unsalted butter
1¾ cups sifted cake flour
1 tablespoon bourbon
Powdered sugar for dusting

Using a mixer fitted with the paddle attachment, mix 1 1/2 cups flour, 3/4 cup sugar, baking soda, baking powder and 1/4 teaspoon salt on low speed to combine. On low speed, add 8 tablespoons butter one piece at a time; continue beating until mixture resembles cornmeal, 1 to 2 minutes. Whisk together eggs, vanilla, 3/4 cup bourbon and buttermilk and add to the flour mixture; beat on medium-high speed until light and fluffy, about 1 minute, scraping sides if necessary. Coat an 8-inch square cake pan with nonstick cooking spray and cut a 16-inch length of parchment paper and fold lengthwise to an 8-inch width and fit into the pan, pushing it into the corners and up the sides; allow excess to overhang the edges of the pan. Use these edges to lift the cake out of the pan. Pour batter into the pan and gently knock the bottom on the counter top to remove any air bubbles. Preheat oven to 325 degrees.

In the same bowl, whisk together the sugars, cinnamon, salt, and butter. Add the flour and bourbon and mix until the mixture resembles a crumbly dough. Pinch off very small pieces of dough, roll them into little crumbs and drop on top of the batter until all the dough is used. (This will be time-consuming.) Bake on a middle rack for 40 minutes, or until the top is brown and springs back slightly when touched. Cool in pan, dust with powdered sugar and lift out before serving.

The Angels' Share

Every bourbon aficionado knows it's a sad fact that for every barrel of whiskey produced, a small portion is lost to the evaporation process. If legend is to be believed, these precious vapors don't just disappear into thin air, but rather make their way heavenwards, to the eager clutches of thirsty angels.

Blue Monday Ice Cream

In 1921 Kentucky native Ruth Hunt began selling the confections her friends and family had raved so much about from a small candy shop in her home. The business took off and in 1930 she moved the store to its current location in Mt. Sterling. Her most famous product would be the Blue Monday bar, a sophisticated treat with a pulled cream candy center and dark chocolate coating. It has been produced for more than 60 years, ever since a traveling minister remarked that he needed a little sweet to get him through his blue Mondays. Here it adds a distinct flavor to vanilla ice cream spiked with a dash of good bourbon. If you can't find Blue Monday bars where you are, use your favorite candy instead.

Ruth Hunt Candy Company
550 North Maysville Road
Mt. Sterling, KY 40353
(800) 927-0302

2 cups whole milk
1 cup granulated sugar
3 large eggs
1 teaspoon vanilla extract
1 tablespoon all-purpose flour
¼ teaspoon salt
¼ cup bourbon
2 cups heavy cream
4 Blue Monday bars, chopped in pieces

Whisk together the milk, sugar, eggs, vanilla, flour, salt, and bourbon in a saucepan over a medium-low heat. Cook until the mixture thickens, stirring often. Remove from the heat and let cool. Whip the cream in a large bowl until soft peaks form. Once the custard mixture has cooled completely, fold in the whipped cream, followed by the Blue Monday pieces. (If there are lumps in the custard, you may want to purée the mixture in a blender before adding to the whipped cream.) Transfer to a 6-cup electric ice cream maker and follow the manufacturer's instructions for making ice cream.

Apple Bourbon Upside Down Cake

Many bourbons display traits of brown sugar, caramel and spices in their flavor and aroma, so they provide a natural complement to the sweetness of apples. For this recipe I like to use a no-nonsense 90 proof bourbon like Ezra Brooks. It's aromatic and extremely affordable, both traits you want to look for in a good baking bourbon.

1 cup unsalted butter, softened,
  plus extra for greasing the pan
½ cup light brown sugar
½ cup bourbon
4 large, crisp Granny Smith apples,
  peeled, cored and thickly sliced
1 tablespoon fresh lemon juice
½ teaspoon ground cinnamon
2 teaspoons salt
2 cups sifted cake flour
1 teaspoon baking powder
¾ cup granulated sugar
2 large eggs, at room temperature
1 teaspoon pure vanilla extract
½ cup buttermilk

Preheat the oven to 350 degrees. Butter a large round, spring-form cake pan. In a medium saucepan, melt 4 tablespoons of the butter over medium heat and add the brown sugar and 1/2 of the bourbon, stirring until the sugar bubbles. Remove from the heat and toss the apple slices with the lemon juice, cinnamon, and a pinch of the salt. Pour the melted butter/sugar mixture into the pan and arrange the apple slices in a spiral pattern around the bottom.

Whisk together the flour, baking powder and salt in a bowl and set aside. Beat the remaining butter in a mixer fitted with a paddle attachment, just until smooth. Add the sugar and beat on medium speed until light and fluffy, about 2 minutes. Add the eggs, 1 at a time, and beat until incorporated. Add the vanilla and reduce the speed to low. Add 1/2 of the flour mixture with the buttermilk and mix. Add the remaining flour with the bourbon and mix. Pour the mixture over the apples and bake until golden and the center springs back when lightly touched, about 35 minutes. Cool on a wire rack for about 5 minutes, then flip the pan over onto a serving plate. Let the cake sit upside down for a moment, then lift off the pan. Serve warm or at room temperature.

Repeal Day Pound Cake

Like a fine wine, every bottle of Evan Williams Single Barrel Vintage Bourbon has a date telling exactly when it went into the oak barrel to age. Each year a new vintage hits the shelves in the best liquor shops in the country, and each year it is met with critical acclaim. It shines with the simple flavors of butter and vanilla in a timeless favorite like pound cake. I haven't found a whiskey that doesn't work well here, so experiment, and see which one becomes your favorite.

1 cup unsalted butter, softened,
  plus additional for buttering pan
3 cups granulated sugar
7 large eggs, at room temperature
1 tablespoon vanilla extract
3 cups sifted cake flour, plus additional for dusting
½ cup buttermilk
1 cup bourbon
2 teaspoons salt

Beat together the butter and sugar in a large bowl using an electric mixer at medium-high speed until pale and fluffy. Add eggs, 1 at a time, beating well after each addition, then beat in vanilla. Reduce the speed to low and add 1/2 of the flour, 1/2 of the buttermilk and bourbon, which have been mixed together. Add the remaining flour, salt and remaining buttermilk/bourbon mixture, mixing well after each addition. Scrape down sides of bowl, and beat at medium-high speed for 5 minutes so the batter becomes rich and satiny. Generously

butter 2 loaf pans and dust with flour, knocking out the excess. Pour the batter into the pans and rap each pan against the work surface once or twice to remove any air bubbles. Place the pan on the middle rack in a cold oven and heat to 350 degrees. Bake until golden and a tooth pick inserted in middle comes out clean, about 1 hour. Cool cakes in the pans on a wire rack and run a thin knife around edges of the cake; invert pan and turn cake out onto rack to finish cooling.

Repeal Day

Enjoy this buttery pound cake on Repeal Day. Conveniently located halfway between Thanksgiving and Christmas, Repeal Day presents a wonderful opportunity to get together with friends and celebrate the end of Prohibition. The ratification of the 18th Amendment on January 16, 1919 ushered in a dark period of American history that banned the sale or transportation of intoxicating liquors that would last until its repeal on December 5, 1933. Although proponents of Prohibition argued that this amendment would eliminate society's ills, respect for the law actually diminished and crime ran rampant. In addition, producers of spirits, wine and beer were forced out of business. It was a sad day for Kentucky, and its bourbon distilleries had to cease production, unless they were one of the handful to receive an exemption from the government to produce whiskey for "medicinal" purposes. Repeal Day – a cause for celebration.

For more information about Repeal Day, go online at: *http://www.repealday.org/*

Orange Bourbon Crème Brûlée

Although both the Spanish and the French take credit for its invention, many thank the English as the inspiration for the sweet, silky concoction with the caramelized sugar crust. Early British students supposedly gave it the original English name that would yield the popular French translation for burnt cream or crème brûlée. This decadent custard has dominated the dessert lists of fine-dining restaurants across the U.S. for the last couple of decades. Here, cream is paired with tart oranges and the sparkle of bourbon.

Juice of 4 large oranges (about 1 cup)
⅓ cup bourbon
¼ cup granulated sugar
8 large egg yolks
½ cup granulated sugar
2 cups heavy cream
½ teaspoon vanilla extract
⅛ teaspoon salt
Sugar for the top

Preheat the oven to 300 degrees. Whisk together the orange juice, bourbon and ¼ cup sugar in a heavy skillet and cook over medium heat until the liquid reduces by half and forms a syrup. Remove from heat and set aside to cool. There should be around ½ cup of syrup. In a large mixing bowl, whisk together the egg yolks with ½ cup sugar until pale yellow and frothy, about 10 minutes. Whisk in the cream, vanilla, and salt. Add the cooled orange–bourbon syrup and continue whisking. Divide the mixture between 6-8 ramekins and transfer the individual ramekins to a large

baking dish. Set on the middle rack of the oven and add enough very hot water so that at least half of the ramekin sits below the surface of the water. Close the door and bake in this bain marie for 15 minutes. Reduce the heat to 250 degrees and cook for another 45 minutes. Remove from the oven and allow the crème brûlée to cool in the water. Once they have cooled, sprinkle about a teaspoon of sugar over the top of each and caramelize under a broiler or with a kitchen torch to achieve the signature sugar crust.

132

Johnny Drum

This dense, buttery cake is named for its star ingredient, Johnny Drum bourbon, which, according to legend, was named for a Civil War drummer boy from Kentucky. The private stock is bottled at high strength and aged for roughly 15 years; like the 12 Year Old, it is the result of bourbon craftsmanship and know-how that has been passed down through five generations of master distillers. Both of them make wonderful additions to this old-fashioned fruit cake, but try your favorite and it's sure to be a hit.

1 cup golden raisins
1½ cups bourbon
1¼ cups softened butter,
    plus extra for greasing the pan
1½ cups sugar
1 cup light brown sugar
5 large eggs, separated
4 cups sifted all-purpose flour,
    plus extra for flouring the pan
1 teaspoon baking powder
1 teaspoon salt
½ teaspoon nutmeg
1 cup chopped pecans
1 cup dried blueberries

Soak the raisins in the bourbon for at least 30 minutes. Using a hand mixer at high speed, cream together the butter and sugars. Add the egg yolks, 1 at a time, and beat well. Mix 3 cups of the flour with the baking powder, salt and nutmeg and add ½ of that to the butter mixture, along with ½ of the soaked raisins

and bourbon. Mix well. Stir in the remaining flour and bourbon and raisins, blending well to remove all lumps. Beat the egg whites to the stiff-peak stage and gently fold into batter. Toss the pecans and blueberries with the remaining cup of flour and fold into the batter. Generously butter and flour a medium-size Charlotte pan. Preheat the oven to 325 degrees and pour the batter into the prepared pan. Bake for 2 hours or until the center of the cake springs back when touched. Turn off the oven and cool for an hour in the oven. Remove from the oven and turn onto a rack to cool completely. When thoroughly cool, store in a tightly covered container in a very cool place.

The Kentucky Bourbon Trail: Wild Turkey

At the Wild Turkey Distillery, visitors can follow the entire bourbon production process from grain delivery to bottling. Aside from viewing the towering column still, they also stroll through timber warehouses and observe the barreling of the whiskey. The no-frills facility occupies an impressive location on the crest of a hill overlooking the Kentucky River.

The distillery was constructed by the Ripy brothers in 1905 and the name came about in 1940 when distillery executive Thomas McCarthy shared some bourbon samples with his friends on a wild turkey hunting trip. The next year, his friends requested more of "that wild turkey whiskey," and a brand was born.

For more information, contact:
Wild Turkey Distillery
1525 Tyron Road
Lawrenceburg, Kentucky 40342
(502) 839-4544

Photo from Wild Turkey Distillery

Photo by James Asher

Photo by David Dominé

Whiskey Truffles

There aren't too many spirits that don't go well with chocolate, and bourbon is no exception. Sweet and smooth, spicy and seductive, smoky and sultry – good bourbon makes chocolate even better. Since the flavor of the whiskey will really come through and shine in these chocolates, choose your favorite sipping bourbon. I like to use Evan Williams Single Barrel or Wild Turkey Kentucky Spirit.

½ cup heavy cream
4 tablespoons salted butter
12 ounces milk chocolate, chopped
12 ounces semisweet chocolate, chopped
½ cup bourbon
Dutch process cocoa for dusting

In a saucepan over a medium-low heat, warm the cream and butter until the butter melts and cream simmers. Remove from the heat. Add the chocolate and whisk until melted and smooth. Stir in the bourbon and pour into a bowl. Cover and freeze until firm enough to scoop out with a spoon, about 40 minutes. Drop by tablespoonfuls onto the bottom of a baking sheet lined with non-stick aluminum foil, spacing them evenly. Freeze for another 30 minutes, until firm but still pliable. Spread the cocoa out on a plate and roll each truffle into a smooth ball with your hands; roll in the cocoa to coat. Return the truffles to freezer for another 30 minutes. Remove and store in a covered container in a cool, dry place.

American Honey Cheesecake

There's nothing "wild" about Wild Turkey's American Honey, a delicious bourbon-based liqueur sweetened with honey. One of only a handful of bourbon liqueurs on the market, this syrupy golden elixir features hints of citrus and caramel that make it a tasty cordial all by itself or sipped with a creamy, sweet dessert like this cheesecake.

6 packages (8 ounces each)
  softened cream cheese
½ cup sour cream
4 large eggs,
  at room temperature
2½ cups granulated sugar
1 cup Wild Turkey
  American Honey
1 tablespoon vanilla extract
½ teaspoon salt
½ teaspoon ground
  white pepper
2 cups graham
  cracker crumbs
2 tablespoons
  granulated sugar
¼ cup melted butter

Use a mixer to beat cream cheese with sour cream, eggs, 2½ cups sugar, American Honey, vanilla, salt, and pepper until perfectly smooth, about 5 minutes at high speed. Preheat the oven to 325 degrees. Mix together the crumbs, 2 tablespoons sugar and butter and press into the bottom and halfway up the sides of a 10-inch spring-form cake pan. Pour the cream cheese mixture into the pan and use several pieces of aluminum foil to seal the bottom of the pan. Set in a pan of warm water on the middle rack of the oven and bake for about 2 hours, or until the surface has cracked slightly and appears firm. Turn off the oven and let the cake cool in the pan in the oven for 1 hour. Take out of the hot water bath and cool completely before removing the side of the pan and serving.

Bourbon Ball Torte

One of Kentucky's most famous confections, the bourbon ball has a rich butter cream center with whiskey and pecans wrapped in a smooth chocolate coating. My favorite bourbon ball is the Happy Ball, a candy made at the Old Louisville Candy Company. The recipe for this rich chocolate cake has been designed to feature them as an ingredient in the filling and as a garnish on the top.

4 ounces bittersweet chocolate
½ cup boiling water
1 cup butter, softened
2 cups sugar
4 large eggs, separated
1 teaspoon vanilla extract
2½ cups sifted cake flour
1 teaspoon baking soda
½ teaspoon cinnamon
½ teaspoon salt
1 cup buttermilk
¾ cup bourbon
2 cups heavy cream
½ cup powdered sugar
16 large bourbon balls
½ cup heavy cream
2 cups semisweet chocolate chips

Break the chocolate into pieces and mix it with the boiling water until completely dissolved. Let cool. Preheat the oven to 350 degrees. Cream the butter and 2 cups sugar until fluffy and pale yellow. Continue beating and add the egg yolks, 1 at a time, until thoroughly combined. Add the chocolate mixture and vanilla and mix well. Sift together the flour, baking soda, cinnamon and salt. Combine the buttermilk and bourbon. To the butter-chocolate mixture, add ½ of the flour and then ½ of the milk, continuing to mix and scrape the sides of the bowl. Add the remaining milk and flour and mix on medium-high speed until smooth. Be careful not to over beat the batter. In a separate bowl, whip the egg whites at high speed until stiff peaks form. Slowly fold the egg whites into the batter and pour into 4 buttered and floured 9-inch round pans. Bake on the center rack for 20 minutes or until a tooth pick inserted in the center of the cake comes out clean. Remove from the oven and cool. Invert pans and turn out cakes.

To begin assembling the torte, use a very sharp, serrated knife to cut off the tops of the cakes to produce 4 even layers. Whip the 2 cups cream with powdered sugar to form very stiff peaks. Chop 8 of the bourbon balls into small pieces and add to the whipped cream. Chill for at least 1 hour so the filling can set up and support the weight of the layers. Brush away excess crumbs from the tops of the cakes and place one layer on a large, flat plate. Top with 1/3 of the filling and spread out to within ¼ inch of the edge. Add the next layer and repeat the process. Refrigerate the cake for at least 2 hours. For the last stage of assembly, scald the ½ cup cream and add to the chocolate chips, whisking until completely melted and smooth. Transfer the cake to a wire rack over a baking sheet and pour the glaze over the cake to coat completely. Cool again, and once the ganache surface has solidified somewhat, decorate the edge with the remaining bourbon balls.

Mix pecans and bourbon in a medium bowl and let soak for at least an hour. Mix the butter and sugar together in a large bowl and add the pecans and bourbon. Chill for 1 hour and roll into ½-inch balls that are placed on a cookie sheet covered with waxed paper. Insert a toothpick into each candy and refrigerate for 2 hours. Melt the chocolate in the top of a double boiler with the cream and stir until smooth. Remove the balls from the refrigerator and one by one, dip each ball into the chocolate and remove. Hold the candy for a few seconds, allowing the chocolate to cool, and place back on the waxed paper. Remove the pick and use a pecan half with a bit of melted chocolate on the bottom to cover the hole and decorate the candy.

Happy Balls!

To pass the attractive façade of the beautiful Victorian mansion locals call the Bishop's Hat House on Third Street in Old Louisville, the average passerby wouldn't suspect that much of a culinary nature was afoot. But, pay a visit to the sharply angled rooms tucked away under the soffits and gables of the roofline and you'll find a sweet secret. It's the Old Louisville Candy Company, where Ron and Jane Harris make Happy Balls. A confectionery creation named in honor of Ron's Aunt Happy, who passed on the original recipe, Happy Balls start off as a mixture of butter cream and nuts flavored with Knob Creek bourbon. They are then hand rolled and dipped, one piece at a time, in Guittard Chocolate, with a pecan half crowning each bonbon.

For information on how to get your own Happy Balls, contact:
Old Louisville Candy Company
1390 South Third Street
Louisville, Kentucky 40208
(502) 637-2227

If you can't get your hands on Happy Balls or other ready-made bourbon balls, try this recipe to make your own:

Bourbon Balls

¾ cup chopped pecans
10 teaspoons bourbon
¼ cup softened butter
3½ cups powdered sugar
2 cups semisweet chocolate chips
3 tablespoons heavy cream
Pecan halves

Ginger Bourbon Lace with Chantilly Cream and Fresh Fruit

Every year since 2002, master distiller Chris Morris has been releasing a special birthday bourbon to commemorate the birth of George Garvin Brown, founder of Old Forester and the first person said to bottle bourbon. Orange-brown in color, it displays a prominent cinnamon-caramel nose that sets the stage for a full taste balanced with flavors of vanilla and apple. It adds the perfect touch to this elegant dessert of delicate lace cookies shaped into cups while still warm and then filled with fresh fruit and sweetened whipped cream. For an extra bit of sweetness, enjoy this with a cordial of Wild Turkey American Honey or Evan Williams Honey Reserve.

½ cup firmly packed light brown sugar
6 tablespoons unsalted butter
2 tablespoons unsulfured blackstrap molasses
2 tablespoons bourbon
4 tablespoons all-purpose flour
4 tablespoons rolled oats
4 tablespoons finely chopped pecans
1 teaspoon ground ginger
1 pinch kosher salt
Chantilly cream
Fresh fruit

Bring the sugar, butter, molasses, and bourbon to a boil over a moderate heat in a medium-size heavy saucepan; stir and boil for 1 minute. Remove from the heat and stir in the flour, oats, pecans, ginger, and salt. Cool the batter for 2 minutes and drop 2-tablespoon portions of dough 6 inches apart onto parchment-lined baking sheets. Bake in batches in upper and lower thirds of an oven preheated to 350 degrees until cookies are flat and have started to sizzle, switching position of sheets halfway through baking. Remove from the oven and let cool until the cookies begin to set up, about 1 minute. While still warm, form cups by draping each cookie over the bottom of an upturned glass to cool. Cool baking sheets and line with fresh parchment for each of the remaining batches. Fill each cup with chantilly cream and fresh fruit and enjoy.

Chantilly Cream

2 cups heavy cream
2 tablespoons
  powdered sugar
1 teaspoon vanilla extract
2 tablespoons bourbon

In a large, chilled mixing bowl, beat the cream, sugar, and vanilla on high speed until stiff peaks form. Stir in the bourbon. Fill each cup with a quarter cup of cream and top with fresh fruit or berries.

142

Index of Recipes